Living Life to the Full

A Guide to Spiritual Health in Later Years

_____

UNA KROLL

continuum
LONDON • NEW YORK

CONTINUUM

The Tower Building, 11 York Road, London SE1 7NX
80 Maiden Lane, Suite 704, New York, NY 10038

www.continuumbooks.com

First published 2006

Unless otherwise stated, scriptural quotations are from the New Revised
Standard Version © 1989, 1995, Division of Christian Education of the
National Churches of Christ in the United States of America.

Whilst the author and publisher have made every effort to clear any
copyright for the book, there may be instances when we have not been able
to trace the owner. In these cases we would be happy to acknowledge any
ownership and correct in future editions.

British Library Cataloguing-in-Publication Data
A catalogue record for this book is available from the British Library.

ISBN: 0-8264-8079-9

Typeset by Kenneth Burnley, Wirral, Cheshire
Printed and bound in Great Britain by MPG Books Ltd,
Bodmin, Cornwall

Contents

114921

For Betty Houghton
and all who have given up their own homes
to live in sheltered or residential care homes

Acknowledgements

This book has drawn on the experiences of many friends, living and dead. I am particularly indebted to Betty Houghton who has shared with me her experiences of later life and moving into residential care. I am grateful to Dilys Lucas and Peter Wilson who have given me permission to tell their stories. I am grateful to the families of Jim Sanders and Bert Jones for allowing me to write about them in this book. I thank my friend Canon Gerald Hudson for profound insights into the effects of disabling illness on the human spirit in later life. Where a story has begun with the name in parentheses the name represents a composite portrait rather than a named individual.

I thank Rabbi Warren Elf of Bury, Lancashire, for his helpful advice on Jewish attitudes towards death.

I thank Joshua Kroll for his permission to describe how he taught his old granny to use text-messaging on a mobile phone and allowed me to retell the story.

I have consulted many experts for factual material, but all opinions in this book are mine alone. They are not necessarily representative of the official views of the Anglican Church.

Acknowledgements for permission to quote from their publications are due to Harcourt Publishers for permission to quote from 'Ithaca', in *The Complete Poems* of Cavafy; to Burns & Oates, for permission to quote from John O'Donohue's article, 'Spirituality and the Art of Real Presence', in *The Way* Supplement; to Victor Gollancz Ltd for permission to quote from *Helen Waddell* by Dame Felicitas Corrigan, OSB; to the

Review of the Spiritual Life, Carmelite Priory, Oxford, for permission to quote from Rabbi Lionel Blue's article, 'Is There Anyone Else Up There'; to New City Press for permission to quote from Olivier Clément's *On Human Being*; to the Cambridge University Press for permission to quote from de Lange's *Introduction to Judaism*; to Routledge for permission to quote from Elizabeth Kübler-Ross's *On Death and Dying*; to the University of Cambridge for permission to quote from the *Cambridge Alumni Magazine*, No. 44 (2005).

Introduction

He who bends to himself a Joy
Doth the winged life destroy;
But he who kisses Joy as it flies
Lives in Eternity's sunrise.

(William Blake, 1757–1827)[1]

To know how to grow old is the master work of wisdom,
and one of the most difficult chapters in the great art of living.

(Henri-Frédéric Amiel, 1821–72)[2]

William Blake's poetic approach to the span of human life, 'the winged life', the life that seems to fly so quickly through earthly time, may defy human understanding. Like many of his sayings, it comes from a mystical apprehension of truth rather than from logical thought. It captures something of the mystery of a joyful approach to the later years of life. It leaves the reader with a taste of hope in 'Eternity's sunrise'.

Henri-Frédéric Amiel,[3] a noted nineteenth-century French diarist, takes a contrasting and more realistic approach to old age. He makes immediate sense, but leaves the reader with the rather stark thought that growing older may prove to be an uphill struggle. Amiel kept a spiritual diary for some thirty-four years. He moved from guilt and self-condemnation towards a growing maturity and happiness.[4]

Blake and Amiel are making statements that express attitudes, both of which need to be addressed in a book about the human spirit in the later years of life. Joy can be 'kissed' at any stage of life, including very old age. Many people in the early years of retirement make as full a use as they can of the joys of 'freedom' from the constraints of paid employment. They continue to seek joy, to taste it, to hold it briefly and to let it fly ahead. Joy beckons right to the gate of death that opens the way towards the sunrise of eternity. Nevertheless, the reality of diminishment that does come to many in their later years, and the universality of death, have to be faced as well.

In many postmodern industrialized societies the reality of death is sometimes put aside. It is ignored, even by soldiers who train to kill with deadly weapons of war, yet they find themselves affronted when some of them die in battle. The media often reduce death to children's war-like games or 'play at death' stories on television and dramatic theatre. So when the reality of death strikes home in a family, or among friends, it comes as a terrible shock. It touches the human spirit deeply, but in the postmodern, post-Christian societies of the northern hemisphere bereaved people less often turn to religion for spiritual help.

It is natural for children and young people to think of themselves as immortal. Adults around them may play into that illusion. Children ask important questions like, 'How old are you, Mum?' 'Are you going to die?' They get reassuring answers like, 'I'm forty years old.' 'I'm going to be around for a long time yet.' If one of them dares to ask, as they will, 'Am I going to die?', the youngster may be told, 'Don't be so silly', or they are reassured, 'Yes, but not for a very long time.'

These answers to such questions, and others like them, are sometimes enough to put them out of young people's heads, but not always. A road accident, a war, a famine, a tsunami disaster, may remind them of the fragility of life. They know that the dead body lying under a crashed car might have been them. They realize that death comes to young and old alike. Since the life-force is strong in youth, they often put such negative thoughts out of their heads. They go on living and behaving as if they were immortal. How else is it possible to account for the fact that, in an age of technological medicine and definitive research, so many children, adolescents and young men and women defy death by smoking? They also take drugs that they know to be life-threatening. 'Dad smoked two packs a day and he lived until he was eighty-five,' they might say to themselves as they finish their first pack of cigarettes around midday. Unpleasant thoughts about how they might die are put firmly to the back of their minds and there they remain, sometimes for a few years, sometimes for many.

'Death is something that happens to other people, not to me', human beings tend to think, until it comes close to them. A sudden illness, or a life-threatening condition in a parent or sibling, makes an individual aware that she or he may be the next person to die. That sharp recognition of reality may come at any time of life, but when it comes it is an important intimation of the fragility of life, and of its mortality. From that point on the 'I' that constitutes the unique self of each individual assents to death, even if momentarily. Death is no longer thought of as something that happens to other people, other creatures. It becomes an important fact in his or her own life.

This moment of awareness may come at any age. Among people who are over eighty at the beginning of the twenty-first century, it is common for it to have come during their late teenage years. Many lost fathers, brothers, relatives and friends in the Second World War. Those who lived near 'bomb alleys' saw houses and lives destroyed in a night raid. Those kinds of incidents brought reality very close at a formative age.

This book's author became an adult during the 1939–45 World War. Her life was touched by an intimate knowledge of suffering and death at an early age. She worked, first as a doctor of medicine, later as an Anglican minister of religion. Dying and death became familiar companions. The emphasis of her work was to preserve life, to alleviate suffering and to walk with patients to the gate of death. Death indeed lay ahead as it does for all human kind but it was 'not yet; not yet'.

The author now lives in sheltered accommodation, one step away from complete dependency or terminal sickness. When she moved away from complete independence it became important to look for 'Eternity's sunrise'. That was when previously accepted ideas about later life and dying and about what might happen after death became challenging. They clamoured for some thoughtful reflection.

The truism, 'We are born but to die', coined by Alexander Pope (1688–1744),[5] an English poet, writer and satirist, in his treatise, *An Essay on Man*,[6] applies to all created matter, including the universe. Individuals, communities and societies have wrestled with the fact of death as they try to make sense of existence. Most people can admit that life on Planet Earth would be unsustainable without the reality of death, decay and nature's recycling of all its resources. They cannot so easily understand why creation exists at all. Human beings have searched for the meaning of existence since the time they became able to communicate. They seek to find answers to the problem of existence that might give meaning to life and death. Questions and answers may embrace an idea of eternity which includes time and space, but goes beyond both. These answers, partial though they are, have given rise to a myriad of religious beliefs about life before, during and after death.

This book is not primarily concerned with the answers to the meaning of existence. It is impossible to prove the rightness of any system of thought or belief. Answers, however clever and carefully constructed, simply either assuage anxiety for a time, or increase doubt. From early history people have come up with answers to the meaning of existence which satisfy some, and fail to satisfy others. In a sophisticated Western society of the twenty-first century many people have decided to stop looking for answers at all. They are content to accept that they are alive. They are also doubtful about the idea of eternal life, if that is interpreted to mean sentient life after death.

People, like the author, who have religious faith, do not much like their innermost beliefs being challenged by negative philosophies. It can be frightening to think that beliefs, and actions based on those beliefs, might be based on false constructions. It is preferable to think that atheists are wrong. It is difficult for people of faith to think that the span of one life is all that there is. They do not like the thought that human beings 'live on' only in the memories of their immediate relatives and friends, or, if they have been famous in their lifetimes, in the biographies that follow their deaths. Many who profess a firm religious faith tend to rely on the support of other people who have somewhat the same ideas.

At some time in their lives, often in their later years, their beliefs may be challenged. Those who cling to religious faith, and refuse to admit doubt as part of that faith, may miss out on a deeper reality than they realize. It is possible to bend the joy of religious beliefs to one's needs and so destroy all joy in the freedom of 'the winged life'. Some cherished religious beliefs can be illusory so one can chase a mirage of one's own making and miss seeing the sunrise that lies at the horizon between life and death. Doubt is not necessarily an enemy of faith. It can strengthen faith.

In her later years the author of this book has re-examined her beliefs. She has learnt to befriend doubt. She has confronted some of the challenges of later life. She has spent the whole of her working lifetime with people, young and old, who are facing dying, death and bereavement. Most of those years have been spent with people who have no religious beliefs at all, but who have definite and unique characteristics as persons. Her experience of working with them suggests that there is an entity called 'the human spirit' that cannot be confined within religious spirituality.

The gift of consciousness together with an ability to communicate thought and feelings constitute the essence of a person from birth to death. That essence makes human beings who they are becoming at each moment of their lives. The human spirit makes people the unique relational persons that they are. So it is the 'human spirit' that is the subject of this book.

Individuals who now live in affluent industrialized societies often live beyond the biblical span of 'threescore years and ten' allotted to them by the Old Testament psalmist.[7] Many people in the northern hemisphere will live beyond 'fourscore years' to a great age. It is not so in other countries of the world. In the southern hemisphere people can only expect to live to half that age.

This book focuses on the experiences of people in later life in industrialized societies because they are the ones who are living long lives and who most need to appreciate the potential of those later years. The later years of life *can* be a particularly rich time of life. People who are older have much to teach young and old alike. This is so, even though a number of older people may end their lives in mute senility. It is so, even though some individuals may be deprived of their dignity by others. It can be true, even when older people are wholly dependent on those who care about, and for, them. Those who face the diminishment and challenges of later years can live life to the full. They can reflect the meaning of their lives. That growing into 'sunrise at the sunset of life' can transcend dying and death.

The book is a guide to living life to the full in the later years of life. A good guide does not spell out every step of the way because explorers always want to make their own discoveries along the way. It offers signposts that give some direction. It describes some of the scenery. There is always something new to discover while travelling.

A Greek poet and sceptic, Constantine P. Cavafy (1863–1933),[8] spent much of his childhood in England. He spent most of his adult life working as a clerk in the Irrigation Office in Alexandria, Egypt. He travelled much. He was a friend of E. M. Forster (1879–1970).[9] His well-known poem, 'Ithaca', uses imagery from the tale of Ulysses' voyage to Ithaca to describe life's journey:

> When you set out on your journey to Ithaca
> then pray that the road is long,
> full of adventure, full of knowledge.
> Always keep Ithaca fixed in your mind.
> To arrive there is your ultimate goal.
> But do not hurry the voyage at all.
> It is better to let it last for long years;

and even to anchor at the isle when you are old,
rich with all that you have gained on the way,
not expecting that Ithaca will offer you riches.[10]

Yes, that is a good way to travel, but on the way those who keep their eyes open may discover more than they expected when they set out.

1

Ageing and the Human Spirit

Let me be your servant;
Though I look old, yet, I am strong and lusty;
For in my youth I never did apply
Hot and rebellious liquors in my blood,
Nor did not with unabashed forehead woo
The means of weakness and debility;
Therefore my age is as a lusty winter,
Frosty but kindly; let me go with you:
I'll do the service of a younger man
In all your business and necessities.

(William Shakespeare, *As You Like It*)[1]

Shakespeare was an acute observer of life as he saw it in his own time. Here in *As You Like It*, Adam, the family retainer, pleads to be allowed to go into the Forest of Arden with Orlando. In this, and subsequent scenes of the play, Shakespeare dwells on the relationship between young Orlando and the eighty-year-old Adam. Adam wants to give his life savings to the young master who is facing poverty and exile. He discounts his age and probably overestimates his strength when he declares that he can 'do the service of a younger man'. Orlando points this out but agrees to take Adam along with him. Once they are in the forest, Adam finds himself exhausted and begs to be allowed to die. The tenderness of the relationship between the old man and his young master comes out in Orlando's words of encouragement: 'Live a little, comfort a little; cheer thyself a little.'[2] Then he leaves the old man to wait for him as he forages for food and shelter for them both. His quest is successful. The old man is welcomed by the Duke in exile, encamped in the Forest of Arden. After that, no more is heard of Adam.

Some Facts about the Ageing Process

People age at different rates. One woman looks and behaves as an old person when she is seventy years old; she sits in a chair and complains vigorously of her aches and pains. Another can be seen striding along the road without a stick at ninety years of age, her eyes so bright with life that passers-by do not notice her creased face and neck. One man decides to give up driving when he is eighty years old; another is still to be found at the wheel of his car several years later. Some people are glad to retire from active paid work at sixty; others are still cooking meals in a convent when they are eighty-five. 'You are as old as you feel' is an aphorism that contains a good deal of truth, although at the time that Mortimer Collins (1826–76) wrote his original couplet he did not coin that phrase exactly as it is commonly used. His witticism could not apply to men and women of today. He wrote:

> A man is as old as he's feeling,
> A woman as old as she looks.[3]
> *(The Unknown Quantity)*

In this twenty-first century it is *not* possible to tell how old a man or a woman is by looking at them. In today's affluent industrialized countries, people dye their hair, inject Botox into wrinkled skin and sometimes have successful plastic surgery to help them to look younger than they are.

What cannot be denied, however, is that people in richer industrialized nations live much longer and have a better quality of health than do people in the less industrialized, poorer countries of the world. A glance at worldwide statistics for 2004 shows that life expectancy at birth for men and women is

highest in Japan, Sweden and Switzerland. It is lowest in
Angola, Mozambique and Zimbabwe.[4] Infant mortality is cor-
respondingly lowest in the northern hemisphere of the
developed world and highest in the southern hemisphere.[5]

These facts invite consideration about the value of a long life.
People in affluent countries, who are now over seventy years
old, have reached the time of which the psalmist speaks in the
poetic cadences of the Book of Common Prayer:

> The days of our age are threescore years and ten; and
> though men be so strong that they come to fourscore
> years: yet is their strength then but labour and sorrow; so
> soon passeth it away, and we are gone.[6]

An eighty-year-old Londoner is unlikely to admit to the
thought that his life might be of more value than that of an
Angolan farm worker who died around the age of thirty-seven.
He cannot measure the value of his long life against the value of
a newborn child who dies within minutes of achieving breath.
Older people can, however, reflect on the experience of a long
life when they have reached an age when they are happy to say
that they are old. Then they may begin to appreciate some
of the advantages of older age as well as to face the various
challenges of diminished strength.

Important Signs of Ageing

Older bodies have certain signs of ageing in common. Skin loses
its elasticity; wrinkles appear. Even facelifts cannot prevent the
appearance of wrinkled skin on parts of the body that are not
normally visible. Hair turns grey, then white; that fact is undeni-
able, for growing hairs will continue to be white at their roots,
even if hair is dyed. Muscles lose some strength; fit or not, older
people simply cannot compete with stronger young men and
women. Brain cells die and are not replaced; the degree to which
memory is impaired is variable, but what is known for certain is
that reaction times at nerve junctions are slowed in old age.

However fit people have been, or however careful to live healthy lifestyles in their older years, some organs, like the kidney, heart, liver, brain and lungs begin to undergo subtle ageing. Consequently, there is some loss of function of some vital organs; that increases with age. The rather dramatic onset of ageing in ovaries, that takes place at the menopause in women, betokens their natural loss of fertility. That happens well before other organs age. In men there is a corresponding loss of fertility, but it is not necessarily so obvious. Relative loss of libido and sexual performance occurs, even when masked in certain individuals by provocative stimuli, change of partners or drugs that enhance potency.

Those changes are common to all ageing human beings. The rest are variable. Many notice changes in the shape of their eyes and begin to wear spectacles. Some can admit to impaired night vision; others observe that their distance judgement is not as good as it was. Some people deny their ageing until they have their first car accident at an advanced age; even then, they are often unwilling to give up the independence that driving a car brings to all motorists.

Many older people begin to have high-frequency deafness when they turn middle age. More people in Western society now seem able to admit to deafness. Many are happy to wear sophisticated digital hearing aids; they use the induction loops that are now available to help them. Some are not. They continue to complain about the 'mumbled speech' of their children and friends. They get irritable when in large groups of people because they make mistakes. They do not like those errors pointed out; sometimes their difficulties cause them to withdraw from company.

The constant wear and tear that joints are subject to during ordinary activities begin to catch up with older people at a variable age. Few people escape osteoarthritis, and its accompanying aches and pains, for the whole of their lives. Some develop osteoporosis and begin to face lives of constant pain.

Short-term memory may become impaired, this time because of the death of cells in the brain. This seldom means that people are descending into the dreaded Alzheimer's disease. Some memory impairment in later life has to be accepted, and managed, if older people are not to be driven to extreme irritability by their naturally ageing brain cells. There are, as will be shown later, some considerable advantages in loss of short-term memory, especially when long-term memory for past events is significantly improved.

Diseases in organs that are due to ageing are common in older people. The weakening of heart muscles can lead to varying degrees of heart failure. The heart no longer pumps so efficiently as it did when a person was younger. The death of cells in the kidneys may mean that they do not work as well as they once did. As the cells and tubules begins to fail the body accumulates fluid. Kidney failure occurs some time before a person dies. Ageing arteries increase an individual's chances of developing a stroke, or heart attack. Narrow arteries in extremities may lead to poor circulation. Older people's brain cells age progressively. This is because brain cells die and are not replaced. Modern science has been able to retard the onset of these ageing processes to a remarkable degree. If human beings live to great age the vital organs of their bodies will begin to die, even before they do.

Some people suggest that personality traits become accentuated in the later years of life. Professional care workers have heard that proposition for most of their working lives. Scientific support is scarce; personal experience has been unclear. Many people have said that as they have grown older, certain traits, which they once observed in their middle-aged parents, have begun to emerge in them. The way they use their hands now reminds them of the gestures of their mothers. The way they think about young people sometimes echoes the way their mother thought when they were young. The way they compare the world of today with the one they knew half a century ago, and saw through their fathers' eyes, may indicate their preference for the 'old ways'. People who are honest with themselves can note all these tendencies in themselves. They may decide to retain fixed attitudes. They may try to go against them, knowing that what was right in their younger years is not necessarily right for them in later life.

Anecdotes abound about ways in which past memories sometimes plague older people. Many people experience guilt and depression about past actions and failures. Guilt is an important problem in older people. It will be discussed in later chapters.

Older people often ask questions about the quality of life they can expect in their remaining years. They also want to know how they can contribute positively to an affluent but ageing society. People who are still fairly active and independent may find themselves having time to reflect on the role of the human spirit in ageing.

The Nature of the Human Spirit as Seen by Former Generations

The human spirit is a difficult entity to describe, even more so if one considers its companion word, 'spirituality'. Everyone uses these words; no one can define them with a precision that finds universal acceptance. Until the twentieth century these words have often been associated with religious concepts.

Some British Christians, who now belong to the older generation, grew up in a classical Graeco-Roman Christianized culture. When they hear the word 'spirit' they often associate it with an ethereal entity, something that is real but different from matter. In their youth the culture was Christian. They can easily make the transition from 'spirit' inside themselves to ideas about God the Holy Spirit. They may have glimpsed the meaning of the Trinity. So they may be able to associate God with the mystery of human existence, especially if they know something of the origins of 'spirit' in Hebrew and Greek.

Many people, however, even committed Christians, do not use words like *rûah* and *pneuma*: wind and breath. Even if they can think of God, the Holy Spirit, as being like a gentle breeze or a breath of pure air, they do not generally experience God in that precise way. God, even if they believe in God, often seems to act without apparent concern for human beings. God's presence operates at an intangible, imperceptible deep level of relationship. Analogies sometimes help. They may, however, hinder understanding.

Thoughts about God as 'Spirit' are typical of people who are now over seventy years of age and who received a classical education. In a post-Christian Western world they do not have the same resonance. God as an abiding presence in baptized Christians, in the Church, is not a reality for the majority of people in present-day societies. Instead, people are familiar with, and vaguely knowledgeable about, other monotheistic religions. They meet with many pantheistic forms of religion, Buddhism and humanism. This knowledge has extended people's views about self-determination and its role in human destiny. Words like 'spirit and spirituality' do not necessarily connect to God at all.

These words, 'spirit' and 'spirituality', need exploring without their religious connotations, whenever people talk about them today. This is not as easy a task as might appear, for to some extent all adults are influenced by their early upbringing. One person may have heard about the Holy Spirit, or the human spirit, during his or her formative years. Another will have only a notion of 'karma', fate or self-determined destiny. For some, the only idea of 'spirit' they have is that it is located in the ego, the 'I' that makes them who they are.

Some people, hearing the word 'spirit' for the first time, associate it with alcohol, that delectable chemical that, if taken in moderation, 'raises the spirits' and takes them into comfortable fantasy. Alcohol may cause drunkenness. Its victims may become totally incapacitated. The phrase 'raising the spirits' implies that the human spirit is an entity. Such an entity may respond to an external agent, such as alcohol, or to an internal movement of thought or feeling.

A more general definition of what 'spirit' means is that it is that core dimension of 'being' that brings living creatures into relationship. Every living creature is dependent on relationship for life. Trees and plants need water, earth and air to live.

Animals need food, protection in immaturity and other creatures to survive. Human animals need all creation, all creatures
and each other if they are to survive birth.

Human infants are born in a state of immaturity. They need
a long period of development before they come to maturity.
They also rely on relationship with all creation, including other
human beings, so that they can thrive and become adults.
Human beings are who they are through becoming. Part of that
becoming depends on their genes; part to their development in
the wombs of their mothers. Part is due to relationships during
birth and formation in childhood. As they mature they are
affected by their past experiences and by their future hopes.
They learn about death. They begin to ask questions about
what happens after death. Human beings are conscious of
time–space relationships as well as interpersonal relationships
and that dimension enters into who a person is becoming.

Relationship then is an inherent part of creation as it exists.
Human beings have highly developed brains. They have developed ways of communication that enable them to relate to time
and space. As conscious creatures they can record thoughts and
feelings in ways that can cross generations. The longing for
relationship with 'the other', be it creation, nature, the environment or other human beings, is an inherent gift of being
born a human being. A person has the potential ability to use
language, thought and memory together. These skills are
related to a sense of history in a time–space continuum. Consciousness is well developed in the majority of adults. They can
share their thoughts and feelings internally with an entity they
call 'self', as well as externally with other human beings. Such
relationships can transcend cultural and linguistic differences.
Some people can communicate across species. People's
thoughts and feelings do not appear to be material; yet their
energy is transmissible through wave forms. They can also affect
matter. Thoughts and feelings are considered to be expressions
of the human spirit, the human personality.

The Human Spirit in Unusual and Exceptional Circumstances

The reality of the human spirit may be clarified by looking at what happens in people who do not have consciousness as well developed as in the majority. There are some autistic children, for instance, who relate only to ritual, or to some objects, rather than to people. Diseases like dementia, or other extensive brain pathology, damage the person's ability to communicate and relate. 'The person I married has gone,' some people say. They are trying to describe what it is like to live with someone whom they knew before that person developed irreversible changes in the cortex of their brain. Yet, as anyone who has cared for an autistic child, or a demented adult, knows, he or she remains a human being. There is still a relationship, even if it is not the one that is desirable. When language, recognition and memory seem to have gone it is still possible for one human spirit to reach out to another, to claim relationship, to empathize. Human beings may not want to do that, or be able to do that, but they have the potential to do so, the desire to relate, because of their species identity.

It is also important to think about what the human spirit might be in exceptional circumstances. Such circumstances exist when a person is permanently unconscious. They can no longer communicate, or take any care of themselves, but their heart and lungs continue to function without external help. Such a person is in a 'vegetative state'. Doctors do not refer to such people as 'human vegetables'. To do so would be to dehumanize that person. It could lead to them treating that individual as a 'class of being' that is not human. It would then be easier to kill that individual without too much difficulty.

When fully conscious people look at an unconscious person their natural tendency is to identify with that person. They are tuning in to a species identity. It makes it difficult for them to deny the humanity of any individual whose thinking brain has been cut off from the vital functions of the brain stem.

Species identity is vital to human solidarity. Once people begin to think of other people as not being fully human, their attitudes change. They may begin to think it right to treat some people as a subhuman class of 'animals' or 'vegetables'. In past history this attitude of mind has operated in subtle, and not so subtle, ways. Mass thinking of this kind can, and does, lead to holocaust and genocide.[7]

The thinking that describes someone as being in a 'vegetative state', rather than as 'a vegetable', recognizes that person's full humanity. The conscious person is not meeting a collection of material atoms and molecules existing in one dimension. He or she is meeting a person who belongs to the human family. That person has worth and dignity within human history. These fully conscious and responsible people recognize the existence of a 'human spirit'. Spirit in this sense is an 'entity' irrespective of any supernatural identity.

The argument outlined here *is* an extreme one. It is an important one to consider at a time when issues such as mercy killing and active euthanasia are being raised in 'civilized' societies. Further discussion will be found in Chapters 2 and 8. The logical result of thinking of anyone at all as 'subhuman', or of describing them as nothing more than a 'vegetable', is one of the reasons why Immanuel Kant's aphorism, 'act only on that maxim whereby thou canst at the same time will that it should become a universal law',[8] is so important. It should be raised in parliamentary discussions on legalizing active euthanasia.

Human Beings in Relationship with Creation, Time, Space and Eternity

Human identity relates to history in time and space. Human beings have language as a species gift. They are able to document their progress in time. Through the gift of consciousness they have also been able to relate to inanimate and animate creation in ways that do not necessarily entail the use of language. They can form relationships. They can pass on the fruits of encounter across cultures and across time. They use music, art, writings to do so. Some people believe that communication can also take place through wave thoughts. These operate at an unconscious level, yet produce effects on the recipients of such thoughts.

Eternity is the dimension of existence beyond time and space. It is the origin of creation, and the future fulfilment of creation (the *telos*). Some people believe in eternal life; others do not. Those who do and those who do not are still inseparable in their humanity. Part of that common humanity expresses itself in ways that suggest that in human personality there is an invisible and intangible element that can help individuals to relate to themselves and to all creation. The human spirit *is* that entity that brings a person into relationship with creation, with historical time and space, past, present and future. It is an essential factor in forming relationships that transcend formal communication. It should now be possible to see how age and ageing relate to that entity through experience.

The Effect of Age on the Human Spirit

Newborn babies are undoubtedly 'spiritual beings'. Located within their genes they have full potential for becoming who they will become As they mature, that potential develops through circumstance and experience in a time–space continuum. 'Cogito, ergo sum' (I think, therefore I am)[9] is not the whole story. Part of that experience, both during and after childhood, comes through contact with numinous or mysterious elements of life. Art, literature, music and drama express those dimensions of life. People who have no contact with religious experience can undoubtedly 'tune in' to the collective emotion and awe that can overcome individuals and groups of people when confronted with the mystery of recognizable transcendence. Rational, or cognitive, relationships, firmly fixed in present time and space, do not sum up the fullness of human experience.

The questions about the meaning of life that many people ask as they are growing from childhood into maturity often disappear in adult life. They are too busy to stop and think. Such questions may not return again if they die suddenly, or at a young age. They return with some force during later life, primarily because of the weakening of the body, the enforced leisure, the waiting in the ante-room of death that are the predominant features of great age. It is a common experience to hear older people saying that they feel remarkably young, and actively interested in life, even when they know that their bodies and organs are decaying. Slowing down in all sorts of ways, they find themselves with more time to think, remember and muse on life than they once had. Some can no longer read or sew. Others cannot hear properly or watch television with pleasure. What most remain able to do, however, is to reflect on their own and other people's lives. Shakespeare, with his acute powers of observation, speaks for those who pass through the seven ages of man and end up unable to reflect. He ends with these poignant words:

> Last scene of all,
> that ends this strange eventful history,
> in second childishness and mere oblivion,
> Sans teeth, sans eyes, sans taste, sans everything.
>   (*As You Like It*, II.vii)[10]

Shakespeare did not reach old age, the age of which he is speaking, before he died, but he certainly penetrated the mind of older people in his plays. In *King Lear* Shakespeare does not praise longevity: he simply describes a way of living with any imprisonment. His words are apt to the imprisonment of older bodies and failing powers. In this passage Lear and his daughter, Cordelia, have been captured. Cordelia utters a lament about the injustice of their fate. Lear contradicts her:

> No, no, no, no! Come, let's away to prison;
> We two alone will sing like birds i' the cage:
> When thou dost ask me blessing, I'll kneel down
> And ask of thee forgiveness; so we'll live,
> And pray, and sing, and tell old tales, and laugh
> At gilded butterflies, and hear poor rogues
> Talk of court news; and we'll talk with them too,

> Who loses and who wins, who's in, who's out;
> And take upon's the mystery of things,
> As if we were God's spies: and we'll wear out,
> In a walled prison, packs and sects of great ones
> That ebb and flow by the moon.
>
> (*King Lear*, v.iii)[11]

Lear is talking to Cordelia as if she were old, which she is not. He is speaking in a way with which many older people can empathize.

There is a real sense in which Cordelia and Lear are one person. In every old person like Lear there is the memory of how they were when they were young like Cordelia. There is a continuity between who one was, who one is becoming and who one will be at the end of life. When the diminishment of old age descends upon all that they have ever been, it is the whole history of humanity that is imprisoned. Cordelia and Lear go together into prison. It is Lear who knows how to live in that state when 'being who you are' largely takes over from the ability to 'do' very much.

Lear asserts that imprisonment of any sort cannot defeat the human spirit. It will continue to sing. The song will come out of the experience of life. He says that the spirit is an animating force in human life. The experience of living life from birth to death prompts people who reach the later years of life to recognize that at times they have not been a blessing to creation. They need forgiveness, not only from their children, but also from all creation. That is why Lear kneels to ask forgiveness. That way, they can live content, and 'pray and sing and tell old tales, and laugh at gilded butterflies'. Being forgiven for the past, they can engage with life from afar. They can even enjoy the preoccupations of those for whom activity is still all-important. That way, but perhaps only in prisons of some kinds during their lifetimes, they can take upon them 'the mystery of things', as Lear suggests to Cordelia. In later years, people can see things about time, space, history and eternity, *as if* they were God's spies. Spies see hidden things. Shakespeare would have known from his own Christian upbringing that God, being all-seeing and all-knowing, does not need spies. God does give human beings, being 'made in the image and likeness of God', the ability to see *as if* they were spies. They can look beyond the obvious surface of life to its core.

If then, as is suggested, the human spirit is that core element of personality that brings human beings into relationship, then 'spirituality' is anything that makes relationship easier. Many people seem to have recognized this. They talk about nature spirituality, New Age spirituality, Hindu, Buddhist, Jewish, Muslim and Christian spirituality. Such descriptions define ways in which particular beliefs, and modes of being, nourish the human spirit. In these ways people have been able to be selective about what suits them. It has made for a plethora of spiritual tools offered for their use. The glut of different kinds of spirituality that are available in the twenty-first century may bewilder some 'postmodern' individuals.

The impact of technology in a sophisticated, industrialized, consumerist, competitive society can affect the human spirit. Society's focus on individual achievement, success and material well-being has swamped many people. Consequently, insights into the human spirit seem to be in danger of being lost. Formerly, they were retained through formal religions. Now, that is not so; not, at least, for the majority of people in such societies. It is important to see whether it is possible to find ways of nourishing the human spirit. One rich resource comes from the experience of an ever-growing number of the older members of societies.

2

Meeting Some of the Challenges of Later Life

Each life is the biography of a hidden conversation
between consciousness, experience and memory.

(John O'Donohue, 1998)[1]

At the turn of the twentieth century, John O'Donohue, the
author of *Anam Cara: A Book of Celtic Wisdom*,[2] wrote an article
on 'Spirituality as the Art of Real Presence'.[3] It needs time and
effort to unpack some of the author's tightly argued ideas, but
they make good sense. O'Donohue follows up the statement
that heads this chapter by saying:

> In and through all that happens, each life strives to become
> present to itself. To gather in the circle of presence is the
> dream of life. This is the arena of spirituality. In and
> through the ceaseless dialectic of consciousness, experience
> and memory a person's spirit expresses itself. The spirit of
> a person is the ultimate and intimate signature of their
> individuality. It is the source from which consciousness,
> experience and memory unfold and the place to which
> they return and gather.[4]

This chapter looks at how certain bodily consequences of ageing
affect the human spirit. Bodily changes include mental and emotional changes. Changes due to ageing are inevitable. Some are
relatively easy to manage. Others are very difficult. Discussion of
each is separate for the sake of clarity. In real life they overlap.

Some Bodily Challenges of Benign Ageing that Affect the Human Spirit

Benign ageing is a natural process. It is not necessarily free from illness. Disease, however, does not imprison the human spirit. Natural ageing is a time when the dance between consciousness, experience and memory can enrich the human spirit. It is a time for enjoyment and sharing with others. Consciousness is not yet dim; experience is rich; long-term memory is keen. It is true that short-term memory tends to be poorer in older people than it was when they were younger. Long-term memory, however, feeds on experience. It offers people an opportunity to reflect on their life experiences.

The ageing human spirit faces challenges. Many of these come from bodily changes. These include mental and emotional changes in later years. As people get older they begin to be aware of 'then' and 'now'. A delightful old man recently said: 'Two years ago I could walk six miles; now, I can only walk two miles.' He was ninety-five years old. Such remarks are frequent among older people because the only way anyone can measure 'now' is by referring to 'then'. Although this person was content with the change in his strength, many people are not. Physical changes can be a source of much frustration in older people. They can remember times in their lives when they were strong, clear-sighted, easy hearing, quick on the uptake. Many older individuals feel young in spirit and thwarted by their ageing bodies. Irritability and anger over quite small issues are common in this age group. Outbursts of real anger can occur even among people who think of themselves as placid and patient. These are distressing. Compassion towards oneself becomes imperative. Equally, younger people can heal old angry people by their compassion.

Memories of 'then' and 'now' may be disturbing. It is easy to compare experience with future expectation. In one of her poems, 'Up-Hill', Christina Rossetti asks, 'Does the road wind up-hill all the way?'[5] She answers, 'yes, to the very end.' Many older people feel that the road seems to run downhill all the way towards death. They dread the possible loss of bodily function, memory, even consciousness. Such negative ideas are a waste of time. The human spirit, trapped in an ageing body, is more than capable of triumphing over disabilities, given half a chance to do so.

The human spirit does not give in easily. It rises to the challenge; not always in a positive way. Frustration can make human beings into 'grumpy old codgers'. The 'fighting spirit' in old people helps them to retain their independence and autonomy. Relatives and friends sometimes find this difficult, but it is a vital part of an older person's well-being. So-called 'oldies' sometimes take calculated risks. They do so, often against advice, so as to do what they still want to do. In the effort to 'keep going', many discover more courage in themselves than they thought they had.

A visit to an old people's home, or the geriatric ward of a hospital, reveals such courage at work. Young visitors' eyes tend to see old people sitting immobile in chairs, often in pain for one reason or another. Visitors may feel afraid. Is this their own future? So they bring flowers, or fruit, ask after the inmate's health, speak cheerily, pick up the washing and leave thankfully after the visit. Many older visitors know better. They dig into their reserves of conscious memory and experience. They elicit tales from the past. They build on those remembered times to evoke courage to live in the present.

Sometimes residents in retirement homes and cottage hospitals are an inspiration to younger people. They can teach others how to live in middle age, and how to grow old gracefully. Younger people may not always want to learn the lessons older individuals have to teach them. If they take time to get past the disabilities, they may reach the spirit of an older person. That spirit is 'the ultimate and intimate signature of their individuality'.[6] The younger person may be astonished by the strength and beauty of that spirit.

Consider a typical visit to a cottage hospital somewhere in Britain. This one happened some years ago. In the first ward there is a seventy-five-year-old man. His arteries have aged more than the rest of his body. He had a lower leg amputated two weeks ago. He is here for convalescence and rehabilitation. He is on crutches, but says that he will walk again. He had a friend of the same age who lost his left leg and did walk again. It hurt. He walked. This amputee intends to do the same. By bedtime he will slide into bed thankfully. The struggle will begin again in the morning.

In the day room there is an eighty-year-old lady with a broken shoulder. The number of falls she has had recently alarms her children. They would like her to move into a nursing home. She will have none of it. She knows that she can only return to her flat in sheltered accommodation if she 'passes a test' in independent living. 'Like a driving test,' her visitor says, who herself remembers that she failed to pass her first driving test at the age of thirty-two. The comment spurs the old lady past the pain in her shoulder. 'I passed my driving test, first time, you know,' she replies. She launches forth into a description of her time in the Second World War when she was a driver in the armed forces. Patient and visitor sit together entranced. Their memories bind them together. The visitor admires the patient's determination to overcome obstacles to her doing what she still wants to do. The older woman had a lively spirit in her youth. She still does.

In the ward, which is home to people who are too ill to go into the day room, is a great old friend. Jim is ninety-two years old. In his younger years he was a well-respected farmer in the locality. Ten years or more ago he had a major heart operation, two years ago a cataract operation. Until last year he cared devotedly for his wife, Gertie, who suffered from Alzheimer's disease. She died in this hospital. Now it is his turn. He is taking a long time about it. His old body is so strong. It will not let him die. He struggles for breath. He hates the oxygen mask that is helping him to keep going. His visitor has known him for sixteen years. She has shared all kinds of tales about his life as a farmer, husband and father. Life since the death of his wife has not been the same. Now he is too ill to speak. She holds his hands. Words no longer seem important. She says that she 'will

be back this evening'. His weary blue eyes reply that he is com-
forted by that thought. She kisses him full on the lips and
departs. Five days and five evenings will come and go before his
release when he will slip from consciousness to semi-conscious-
ness and finally into a coma. Every day his visitor will come and
hold his hands. Every day she will kiss him, all need for cautious
propriety gone, spirit meeting spirit.

Benign old age is like that. It is a mixture of facing reality
with courage, black humour and tender communication. It is a
way in which the human spirit can teach another person how to
face old age and death.

Some Bodily Challenges of Malignant Old Age that Affect the Human Spirit

Old age is not always so kind. 'Rage, rage against the dying of
the light',[7] Dylan Thomas (1914–53), the Welsh poet, wrote
when his father was dying. He was still a young man when he
wrote that poem. It *is* like that for many older people. Malignant ageing *is* terrible to meet. The destruction of the
personality, that is sometimes a feature of people's later years, or
of terminal illness, is dreadful to watch. Pain, sepsis, chronic
failure of heart, lungs, kidneys, nervous system in all its many
variations, can test the metal of many old people and their
caring relatives and friends.

One person to whom this happened was a Christian who was
dying from a brain tumour. She was comparatively young,
being no more than seventy years old at the time of her terminal
illness. She and her friends had been colleagues in the 1970's
movement to get the British Parliament to pass legislation to
begin to abolish Sex Discrimination.[8] She was one of the
staunchest Christians her contemporaries knew. She invariably
had a sound theological argument to defend her views on almost
any ethical issue. People respected her views even when they
did not agree with them.

One of these friends was about to visit her in hospital. A
mutual friend came to her in some distress. She said that Mary

(that is not her real name) had lost her faith. 'Never', the friend thought to herself, as she opened the ward door and went to find her. 'Not Mary!' It was, however, true. Mary was locked into atheism as firmly as she had formerly been locked into her Christian faith. She railed against God. She refused to see any clergy. She hurled abuse at her visitor.

Mary's whole personality seemed to have changed. Later the visitor said that she had tried to find the person she had known. Mary did not seem to be there. Although the visitor saw her friend several times before she died, that state of mind did not alter. The dreadful end to this woman's life can teach much to those who are willing to accompany dying people.

The witness to this death learnt that religious faith can be a finite entity. At least, it is in some people. So, for that matter, is atheism. Both can change beyond recognition under the impact of a life-threatening illness or old age.[9] Thankfully, she was young enough to realize that her own spirit might wither in old age, or under the impact of a terminal illness. She needed to accept the possibility of changes to her personality. The young visitor also had to learn that there is a precious element in humanity that bonds individuals to one another. She needed to learn to trust without undue anxiety. This episode taught her to surrender to future possibility, whatever that was.

That was the lesson that Mary taught by her dying. Later, the memory of Mary's dying helped the visitor and others when they too were assailed by doubts about faith. Talking things over, they realized that if their dread of being senile in old age and losing their faith came true, they would not be quite alone. The collective strength of the human spirit would be with them, either from fellow patients, or from those who watched and waited. Many people who were Mary's close friends at the time learnt to let go. They let go of fixed beliefs about faith. They learnt to trust whatever the future held.

This patient's impairment of brain function came from a brain tumour. A more common cause of impaired brain function in later years comes from repeated small strokes, from Alzheimer's disease and from other causes of mental deterioration. These can be malignant in every sense of the word. Many patients in the early stages of such diseases know that their thinking abilities and memory are diminishing. This causes distress. Relatives, friends and professional carers have to watch helplessly as people lose the ability to care for themselves. Some patients just sink gracefully into total dependency on outside help for feeding and all forms of personal care. Others, however, wander by day and night, become wildly aggressive and cause mayhem both within their homes and outside. They become unrecognizable as the people they once were. Many people who care for such patients feel that personality and the human spirit are synonymous. Some do not. They think the spirit is still there, hidden beneath the wrecked brain. The care of the human spirit in such adverse circumstances will be more fully discussed in Chapter 5.

Meeting the Bodily Challenges of Later Years

The ability to embrace future possibility, whether achieved quickly or slowly, is a gift that often comes to older people. It can act as a tranquil companion to their final years. It sets older people free to enjoy the 'present moment'. Those present moments may lie in sleepy memories of the past and in rich dreams. The sight of a spring daffodil or tulip may give special delight to an older people who know that they may not see another spring. Such a 'present moment' may come from telling stories as if they had never been told before. Doubtless those who tell them will promptly forget they have told them. The stories will be repeated many times. Other moments of delight may come from a nip of whiskey, a cup of tea or a crumpet. Neither past nor future can compete with that precious 'present moment' in which the human spirit can dwell in joy and peace. Sometimes, when a long-married couple finds that one of them is going to die before too long, they learn to live to the full in the 'present moment' that they know will never come again. Death is inevitable, and they know it. They just want to live each moment, each hour, each day, as fully as possible, whatever the next day might, or might not, hold. They no longer wait for birthdays to share gifts. They no longer wait for tomorrow to say how much they love each other. They no longer worry about tomorrow at all. They are content to live in the present moment.

It is not easy to make such assertions, or to invite others to embrace the unknown that lies ahead of human beings. Embracing the unknown is a gift that seldom comes all at once. Older people are privileged to have time to face the diminishments of their later years. Once accomplished, once people have accepted that they *are* old, that they *are* waiting to die, they can reach a kind of freedom. That freedom enables them to enjoy life as it is. Much fun remains. The most indelicate disabilities can provoke laughter. Relatives, friends and carers may offer a great deal of love. Acceptance of that love is a gracious act.

It would be foolish to say that *all* older people reach this state of mind. Some people who are 'ornery' when young will remain disgruntled in their old age. Some will refuse the challenges that come with old age and continue to pretend that they are young. Some insist on their own way to the detriment of others. Some always seem to ask for what they want at the least convenient moment. Older people are often distressed to find how ungracious they can be in old age, how irritable they are with the normal frustrations of life, how foolish they are at putting things in places where they know they can find them again. Now they cannot. They need reassurance rather than criticism or condemnation, but they may not get it. Many people, however, given half a chance, do rise splendidly to the challenge of their aged bodies.

Challenges that Come from Other People and Adverse Circumstances

A major challenge of people's later years comes from the way in which younger people treat older people. Many older people seem to be less successful at countering the views other people have of their old age than they are about their own bodies.

Unfortunately, society, in the shape of older people's immediate family, friends and carers, may miss the vitality of spirit and wealth of experience that lies before them. Older people look old; they *are* old. In materialistic and consumer-oriented societies they are past their 'sell by date'. Accordingly, they are sometimes treated as if they were useless, or heading for senility. Older people cannot triumph over the disabilities of age unless they are given a chance to do so by younger people.

Older people's perceptions of how other, generally younger, people see them can lead to a great deal of frustration. Their reactions to younger people's views may lead to danger. They may, for instance, react strongly to a suggestion that they are no longer fit to drive a car. Woe betide the relative who points out the damage on the side of the car or the broken headlight. Friendship may falter under the strain of comments about a recent 'near miss'. Sometimes this kind of conversational exchange of views can lead to further accidents because the older person is too stubborn to stop driving.

On the other hand, younger people may seriously underestimate the strength and abilities of older people. Younger relatives and friends may try to limit the activities of older relatives and friends. They may discourage them from travelling, or from doing anything unusual, like giving a lecture. It is, of course, tempting fate for any older person to accept engagements a long way ahead. Older people may feel pleased when they are asked to give a lecture on a familiar topic to a professional audience. They accept with alacrity. By the time of the lecture they may well may feel very different. They may then realize how out of date they are and begin to panic, but illness may intervene. If it does, they are spared the frustration of having to give a less than adequate lecture. If it does not, people may be kinder about the lecture than the old person is in his or her mind.

Worst of all, perhaps, is the frustration of losing independence in old age. Retirement from cherished work may produce less frustration than other losses. Many older people suffer greatly when they can no longer drive. Later they may not be able to travel on public transport; they can no longer shop for themselves. These commonplace companions of old age, together with increasing inability to read, hear, or write a decent hand, constitute some of the real frustrations of old age. Few people think about these disabilities until they catch up with them. When they do, most will meet some real resistance in themselves. They may also feel some antagonism towards those who are eager to help them.

'Let me get up on my own,' someone recently said to a friend who was rushing towards her to help her up after a fall. She did not have the breath to tell her friend that if she was lifted by the shoulders it would cause severe pain to a broken shoulder that had not healed properly. The jolting pain that accompanied the friend's kind action produced an ill-tempered remark. Concealing that pain, through being too proud to disclose it, made the old lady displace her anger on to the shoes lying on the floor where she had stumbled. She gave them a good kick, only to be reprimanded for leaving them in a place where she might stumble over them. 'I know,' she said in a cross voice, and then scolded herself for being such an unpleasant and ungrateful old lady.

Guilt over one's behaviour is a torment in the later years of life. There is so much time to think about the past. Past failures rise up to confront older people. It is so easy to be sucked into the feelings that caused rupture of good relationships in the past. Clouded memories, bewilderment and sorrow make healing difficult. So often the people concerned have either moved away, or have died. There appears to be no chance of repairing the relationship. Common sense can tell the guilty person that it is time to move on, to forget the past. The haunting may not go away so easily. Christians are particularly susceptible to this kind of guilt.

Equally, old resentments crowd in on the long days that many older people spend alone. Someone may have thought he or she had forgiven past hurt. It is painful to discover that the hurt, even the desire for revenge, is still there. Older people sometimes feel consumed by rage when painful incidents go round and round in the mind. Bodily weakness makes this kind of frustration hard to bear. Older people can find themselves in a rage about nothing at all. The real reason for their almost uncontrollable anger possibly lies elsewhere, probably in the past. It can be a great relief to remember the cause of such unexpected and disproportionate anger.

Those who care for older people need to understand these assaults of conscience and feelings. Treatment for guilt, depression and resentments of various kinds may be needed. Some of these treatments will be discussed in Chapters 5 and 6.

Meeting the Challenges that Come from Frustrations and Adverse Circumstances

The frustrations of old age that come from other people and from adversity *are* a challenge. Meeting them depends partly on how people met frustration when they were younger. It also depends on how help is offered by younger and more able people. A personal memory reminds me of a time when an arthritic hip was disabling. Standing was fine. Walking with a limp was possible. Sitting down was reasonably comfortable until the time came to stand. That was very painful. One day need overcame residual pride: I asked for help and was gently lifted to my feet by two strong men. That help was offered on many other occasions afterwards. The men who offered that help treated those occasions as if it was their privilege to enable an older person to continue to work. Eventually a hip replacement restored independence. Such kindness is remembered. Those to whom such help has been given grow in gratitude. They are also more able to ask for help when they need it in future.

The human spirit *is* challenged by frustration. People find victory in stern realism. They may grow in humility. They may develop a grateful heart. Victory comes through acceptance without surrender. When blindness comes, for instance, it may be possible to adapt to pleasurable listening. When deafness prevents communication, it may be possible to learn to lip-read. When eyes and ears fail there is still touch and the precious communication that comes from love.

The most frustrating situations in old age come from the loss of the ability to communicate at a conscious level. This inability to communicate in the usual way affects both patients and those who care for them. It is not known exactly what happens when a person is unconscious. Some of those who care for unconscious patients believe that the human spirit remains able to communicate at a transcendent level, even when the ordinary means of communication become impossible. There is some supporting evidence for this conviction. In this century Dr Menon, a Cambridge trauma specialist, carried out a brain scan on one of his patients in a deep coma. He wrote: 'The MRI scans mapping blood flows to the part of her brain associated with face recognition showed that she could recognize human faces known to her.'[10] That patient was diagnosed as being in a 'vegetative state'. She eventually regained consciousness. Such research is in its infancy. The subject is controversial. Some neurologists would say that the diagnosis was wrong, or the term misused because she was temporarily unconscious. By definition, people in 'persistent vegetative states' do not recover.[11]

When coma supervenes in the final stages of life a person usually dies without being able to speak or show evidence of consciousness. Experience suggests that very ill, semi-comatose people can communicate strong emotions to others. Emotions can sometimes transcend words and gestures, and even touch. If someone who is dying is afraid, then love can meet that fear and cancel it out to allow the person a peaceful death. Some people deny that this can happen. Others do not. They would state that the human spirit can communicate spirit to spirit at a deeper level than consciousness.

The Art of Growing Older

It is very important for conscious and reasonably well old people to be able to relate in positive ways to those who care about them and for them. One of the arts of being older is to learn how to react to other people's tactless remarks. Another is being able to receive help from others. Yet another is to ask directly for what one needs.

The later years of life are often difficult periods of life. They call for discernment about oneself. They call for patience with other people. They call for gratitude even when the older person resents the fact of having to accept help. There is a famous seventeenth-century Nun's Prayer.[12] Whoever wrote it must surely have known how difficult it is to get older. Part of the prayer asks God, 'Restrain me from craving to straighten out everybody's affairs.' It goes on: 'With my vast store of wisdom, it seems a pity not to use it all, but thou knowest Lord that I want a few friends at the end.' These sentiments seem to collude with the habit that younger people in Western society have of discounting the opinions of older people. Many people, especially those who are feminists, rebel against that habit. At the end of the prayer, however, even they may find themselves in full accord with the writer:

> Keep me reasonably sweet; I do not want to be a Saint — some of them are so hard to live with — but a sour old person is one of the crowning works of the devil. Give me the ability to see good things in unexpected places, and talents in unexpected people. And give me grace, O Lord, to tell them so.[13]

Family doctors often feel joy when they visit some of their old 'shut-in' patients. There are a number of older people about whom such doctors speak with gratitude. They make a deliberate effort to visit such patients when they are low in spirits. On opening the door the patient will greet them with affirmative words: 'How good to see you doctor: how are you?' That kind of statement may come from someone who has been bedridden for twelve years. Someone who is dying may say that. An old man who is caring for an incontinent and senile wife may open the door in that way. These people do not deny their suffering. They need help and friendship from their doctors, but they know how to go out of themselves towards other people. It makes it possible for the doctor to sit down, and, for a few minutes, talk about everything under the sun. There might be some shared memories from the past, some word of wisdom about the state of the world, some black humour about old age. Such older people always show interest in their visitor. A family doctor who has such patients is fortunate. Eventually, he or she will turn to the reason for the visit and offer advice. In many instances the patient knows better than the doctor that very little can be done to improve matters for them. Family doctors who still visit patients, and who find the time to do this, will usually leave the house feeling better than they did when they knocked on the front door! Such is the effect of meeting 'reasonably sweet' people of any age.

One of the ways of growing in patience and compassion when people are older is for them to keep interested in all that is going on around them. Grandchildren are specially helpful towards older people. They will laugh kindly when the grandparent gets into a muddle trying to send text messages on the mobile phone. They will, with remarkable patience, teach the older person how to do it. They greet the first successful text message to them with rejoicing. They suggest new tricks that can be learnt. 'That's enough for one day,' the older person might say. The grandparent will put away the mobile phone with relief and plunge into the grandchildren's latest interests.[14]

Middle age is the best time to cultivate an interest in what younger people are doing and achieving. Human beings need to learn that art before they retire, rather than afterwards. Once they reach middle age many people will have achieved most of what their ambition has desired. If they have not, it is too late to be sour about unachieved goals. Middle age is the time to start 'letting go' of power of all sorts. It is the time to practise 'letting go' of responsibilities and status in one's communities outside one's working life. Later life is the time to share wisdom with those who are much younger than they are, to encourage them, to support them through difficulties, to empathize with their struggles and frustrations. Fully retired people often find these outside interests and relationships with younger people become a precious pleasure. Such relationships are satisfying. They help older people to avoid becoming sour and resentful.

Support for younger people, new ventures, changes that suit their generation rather than that of the older person, is an important feature in 'sweet' old age. Older people can affirm the good things that young individuals achieve. They do not need to think that past generations were the best in history. Supportive conversations of this kind will sometimes enable younger generations to listen to the wisdom that comes from consciousness, experience and memory.

Younger people also have a responsibility towards older people. In the current climate of many industrialized countries old people are too often regarded as a 'problem' rather than as an asset. This is reflected in corporate attitudes that sometimes find expression in legislation.

Challenges that Come from Corporate Social Attitudes Towards People in Later Life

Legislation, or impending legislation, often reflects social attitudes towards people in later life. In an industrialized country of the northern hemisphere the message goes something like this:

> You are considered to be old when you begin to draw your pension. Since people in today's industrialized societies are living longer and longer, we may raise the age at which you will stop work. You must now plan for your pensions, as we are unlikely to be able to give you enough to live on when you reach old age. We are also unlikely to be able to find you a hospital bed, or a nursing home, when you are old, especially if you are poor. Yes, we have declared ourselves to be a 'welfare state', but you really must understand that you are unproductive in our society. We are sorry that you are old. We will give you all some extra help with heating. We will supply you with free entertainment on television. If you can still travel, we will give you concessions on public transport. Oh, yes, and we

are thinking about your dying. In future you may be able to choose to terminate your life; people already do in some other sophisticated countries in Europe. Until then do your best to keep out of sight. Be thankful for small mercies and pray for a speedy, pain free and happy death.

That may seem to be a cynical way of describing a modern society's attitude towards old people. It is not, however, an attitude that would be unfamiliar to most older people, some of whom have organized themselves into collectives. They are trying to obtain more justice for older citizens. It may be regrettable that charitable organizations and campaigning bodies, such as Age Concern,[15] have to stand up for the needs of disabled and older people. It is necessary, because negative attitudes towards older people and non-productive, low-income individuals and families have crept into industrialized societies.

The 'welfare state' that came into Britain after the Second World War may now seem outmoded and obsolete. It is open to fraud and unmerciful exploitation. The creeping indifference of the strong towards the weak, the non-productive members of society, young and old, indicate that society has begun to lose faith in human nature. Such a society sees merit only in productivity and success. In a highly competitive world such attitudes override the natural compassion of the human spirit. Postmodern citizens in affluent countries may find themselves living, not only in a post-Christian state, but in a state that is indifferent to the spiritual needs of humanity.

It is unfortunately true that organized religions have now lost their influence on most people in society. This has happened because the Church and some other faith communities no longer seem to resonate with the needs of the human spirit. That does not mean that those needs do not exist. They do. As John O'Donohue says, the human spirit 'is the source from which consciousness, experience and memory unfold and the place to which they return and gather'.[16] He also says that:

Spirituality is then the awakening, articulation and integration of the diversity of possibility and presence within us. True spirituality is the continual dawn where illumination unveils the thresholds where darkness and light, memory and possibility, divine and human are sistered.[17]

In Chapter 6 the role of faith in winning victories over the difficulties of older age will be discussed in the context of the way people make important choices in later life.

Meeting the Challenges of Corporate Social Attitudes Towards People in Later Life

Older people do have important contributions to make to the conversations that stem from consciousness, experience and memory that are going on in today's world. The contributions of elderly citizens are important precisely because they are living in the sunset of their lives. Many of them can see the dawn of a better way of life, if not for themselves, then for those who will be alive after they are dead. Lively opposition to negative social attitudes towards older people is needed. This will be discussed at greater length in Chapter 7 on Ageism.

Is there a spirituality of ageing? Yes, old age is a time when consciousness, experience and memory cohere. Older people *can* contribute to the future of humankind. Spirituality can provide tools that can meet challenge, from within, from close relatives, carers and friends, from society as a whole. People can then go on to meet those challenges by living as if their tomorrows were endless, but also as if this 'present moment' was the last they will have on this earth.

3

Living Life to the Full through Finding Freedom in Later Life

'You are old, Father William,'
the young man said,
'And your hair has become very white;
And yet you incessantly stand on your head –
Do you think, at your age, it is right?'
(Lewis Carroll, *Alice in Wonderland*)[1]

Older people often feel younger than they are. Sometimes they behave outrageously and stand on their heads. 'Mutton dressed up as lamb', is one of the comments that pursue an elderly lady who dares to wear teenage clothes. 'Do you think that's wise?', another person might hear when he tells a friend of his plans to visit the Taj Mahal. The reply might be predictable: 'No, but it's something I want to do before I die.' These people are saying by their actions that they know that they are older, but they are not going to surrender before they have to. They will accept certain bodily limitations; they will not allow themselves to be incapacitated prematurely.

The Freedoms that Come During Early Retirement

Retirement age brings with it certain precious freedoms. Within reasonable and health limits most old people are able to enjoy the early years of their retirement. There is freedom from dressing to please, but plenty of opportunity to wear what one likes. There is freedom from one kind of ambition, that of carving out success, but ample room for taking calculated risks. Some people do make foolish use of their freedom; they put other people's lives at risk because of their irresponsibility, but that is exceptional. Older people's time is their own. They can choose to do what they like, perhaps for the first time in their adult lives. A man who hates retirement, and chooses to return to part-time work, is still a person who has the freedom to make that choice. A woman who decides to undertake an Open University Course at the age of eighty knows that she may not live to collect her degree. She wants to stretch herself and knows she will find pleasure in doing that.

Another freedom that comes with retirement is the relative freedom from the anxieties that come directly from employment. Anxiety may come for other reasons but it no longer comes from work situations. Mistakes no longer matter; there is no one in authority to notice them. Getting to work on time is no longer important. When there are no colleagues to upset there is no need to feel guilty. Initially, these freedoms may go unnoticed. Later they are a considerable relief.

People have particular ways of dealing with retirement. Many people travel. Others pursue learning or skills they have always wanted to acquire, but never had time to take up when they were younger. Visit any fitness centre during normal working hours; you will see plenty of grey heads working hard at keeping fit. The University of the Third Age[2] attracts many people to its courses. They enjoy the course; they meet other interesting people. The sessions are tailored to meet the needs of older people.

One of the delightful freedoms of old age comes to many people when they discover that they are no longer able to hold several thoughts in their heads at one time. Initially, they may feel irritable. People tend to look back to the time when they were younger and could manage to keep several themes clear in their heads. Sometimes, if they can accept the limitations that ageing brings, they can see the value of only focusing on one thought or one activity at a time. That acceptance sets them free to enjoy that one thing they can do at that particular moment. They can feel satisfied with that immediate thought or activity. Living at a slower pace adds to the pleasure of the present moment.

Some loss of short-term memory is normal in older people. One way of dealing with it enjoyably is to look back to the past with the help of photographs. Older people, even those in early retirement, may not be able to remember other people's names very well. That is frustrating, but they are likely to recall memories when they see old pictures from years ago. Some older people build up a 'memory box'.[3] This can be an old shoe box, or something more handsome. Into the box they collect special photographs, scraps of poems, letters and significant dates from their younger lives. These precious memories can go everywhere with them even when they have to descend to living in one small room.

Long-term memory, as opposed to short-term memory, is usually good in later life. Telling stories to children and grand-children is another valuable freedom of a person's later years. Younger relatives and people who care professionally do not always understand this necessity for older people to relive the past. Too often, they are cut off when they begin to tell tales of their past lives. 'You've told us that, Dad,' the children might say, when their father begins yet again to tell of past deeds, joys and pains: or they look vaguely bored. If they had listened, however, they might have seen certain aspects in their elder's behaviour that could help them to understand themselves. They would also affirm the older person's worth by sharing with him or her memories of younger days. That affirmation of who people once were is important to their sense of self-esteem when they are older and are less active.

Caring agencies, particularly those who help people with early Alzheimer's disease, know the value of eliciting 'tales from the past' and of 'memory boxes'. If living in today's pain, today's severe bodily limitations, today's misery, is too awful to contemplate, then it would seem to many elderly people to be good to live in the present moment of years gone by.

After retirement, time has a different meaning than it did when people were young enough to work gainfully. A precious freedom comes with the realization that time is no longer constrained by employment. Older people, for instance, quite often spend time in hospital waiting rooms. 'Waiting does not worry me at all,' one old friend recently said. 'I speak to other people. I take a book to read, settle to it happily and the time passes quickly. That was not true when I was working as a social worker; then I would be anxious about those who needed my services. Of course, it is true that seriously ill people of any age fret if they have to wait for four hours or so in a busy accident and emergency hospital centre,' she said. 'I am not that ill; I positively enjoy my hospital visits.'

British society has been good to older people in a rather paternalistic way. People of pensionable age can enjoy discounted fares, or even free fares. Many can remain active for longer than their predecessors. Some older people cannot manage buses, trams and trains. They cannot afford taxis. 'Ring and ride' services enable them to travel 'door to door' to go shopping, to go to church, even to go visiting. Society is more compassionate to older and disabled people than it used to be. Access to shops, cinemas, theatres and many other public places is easier. Induction loops make it easier for deaf and hard-of-hearing people to follow what is happening. There are even parks that provide special areas of scented flowers so that blind people can enjoy them.

The Freedoms that Come in Very Old Age

In time older people become very old. It is difficult to define an age when that becomes apparent. Often the process is gradual. An accident, a change in circumstances or a bereavement may sometimes precipitate the change. Then, quite quickly, people start to feel old as well as to look old. Sometimes they protect their energy to harvest it for something they really want to do. The disabilities of very old age may be the time when certain freedoms, such as driving a car, or going on high mountain expeditions, have to be abandoned. Defiant rebels may put other people's lives at risk.[4] Those who know they are old, and can acknowledge it, still have a great deal to teach others about living full lives within the boundaries of achievable activity.

Paradoxically, the knowledge that time is limited can also make people reckless, especially if they have no dependent relatives. As has already been said, older age can be a time for going on adventures, defying illness or death, or undertaking something they had never been able to learn when younger. Their relatives, friends and carers may demur: 'You are being irresponsible.' Yes, of course, it would be irresponsible if, for instance, an elderly person insisted on driving at 70 miles an hour for six hours. It *is* foolish not to take rests. The driver's life is then at risk. Other people's lives are also put in danger.

Most elderly people, however, are not irresponsible. They take calculated risks. They know that for them the quality of life is more important than its length. Some, perhaps many, also know how easy it is to lose confidence in one's abilities in later years. Getting on a bus after a hip operation may be daunting. Going out in the evening may be nerve-racking. People who are deaf or blind may not enjoy excursions as much as other people think they should. If people do it at all, they do it to defy their natural reticence in order to stretch themselves, or to ignore their natural desire to withdraw from company. They may also choose to do whatever it is they want to do to enjoy life to the full despite their obvious limitations. They have accepted that their lifespan is limited, that they are close to death, but they are determined to resist stagnation and all that destroys their humanity.

No Surrender: the Spirituality of Resistant Acceptance to Physical Disabilities

The human spirit will thrive if it refuses to be defeated simply because certain freedoms have to be relinquished. The spirituality of later life consists in the art of living in the present moment to the fullest of one's abilities. That art sets people free to live their lives to the full in the present moment. They then live in 'resistant acceptance'.

Resistant acceptance means that people accept the limitations of old age, but remain determined to live to the limit of their abilities. Acceptance of this kind does not submit to old age. Instead, it helps people to learn to bypass the disadvantages of disability. Older people are not the only ones to display this attitude of mind and spirit. Many younger disabled people, handicapped people and those in trouble challenge all kinds of adversities.[5] 'Resistant acceptance' is, however, an important attitude to cultivate in older age. Moreover, sometimes younger people can learn from watching how older people live.

In the first quarter of 2005, the BBC profiled Father Cyril Axelrod, a Roman Catholic priest, who had been born deaf.[6] This disability gave him great empathy with other deaf people. As a young man he had established deaf schools in Macao and in South Africa. In his late middle life, while working in China, he became blind. This disability tormented him because it meant he had to stop his secular work. He felt cut off from people by his double disability. He could have sat down and accepted this frustrating isolation. Instead, he totally accepted that he was severely handicapped. He bypassed his sensory disabilities by learning massage. Father Cyril used touch to communicate with seeing and hearing people. He strengthened his bonds of empathy with other deaf-blind people. He became a profes- sional masseur, then took Holy Orders. He is the only deaf-blind priest in the world.

It was awesome to watch this man. He relied on the deaf- blind alphabet spelt out on his hands by gentle helpers. He sensitively placed the Holy Communion wafers into the hands of his congregation. Those who watched this programme saw the essence of resistant acceptance. Father Cyril had fully accepted his disabilities. He overcame them by bypassing them. He had found a way that brought him the satisfaction of being able to help his fellow human beings.

Writing about the spirituality of old age means that one is necessarily writing about 'the spirit of a person that is the ultimate and intimate signature of their personality'.[7] It means looking for those elements in human beings or in their environment that enable people to express their personalities. The story of the deaf-blind Roman Catholic priest is a story of an exceptional person. In different ways, though, it is possible to find that sort of determination in many people. Another story about a real person illustrates this idea of 'resistant acceptance'. This time it concerns a friendship which started when the author met Dilys in her late seventies. She is now in her mid-nineties.[8]

No Surrender to Imprisonment in Physical Disabilities

Dilys was an active person. She took her beloved dog out every day. She was trim; she wore smart clothes, walked on high heels and was what older people would call 'soignée'. She wore her make-up and accessories with elegance. She was full of life and enjoyed some rich friendships. On Sundays she would walk down to church and greet her fellow Christians with a radiant smile. At the proper time of each year she would approach everyone for money for Christmas flowers; it was almost impossible to refuse a donation.

Dilys concealed the extent to which she had to work hard to keep up her appearance. Friends and fellow worshippers met her where she wanted to be. Eventually she found it all too much for her, so she quietly retreated to her own home. She always left her front door open during the day: those who wanted to 'drop in for a chat' could do so.

It was always a pleasure to visit Dilys. She presided from an armchair in a small room. She was surrounded by beautiful objets d'art. She would talk animatedly about them, or anything else. She tried to conceal her suffering.

A few months ago Dilys was noticeably weaker. She could hardly walk. She had accepted her infirmities, but was still looking for ways round them that would keep her spirit alive. 'I do a crossword every day,' she said. 'It keeps my brain going. I can't look after my little dog anymore. The kind woman who looks after her now brings her to see me most weeks. You are kind to come and see me.'

For years now, Dilys has firmly resisted going into an 'old

people's home'. She has fought to stay in her own home, even to the point when she exasperates some of her relatives and close friends. She knows that she is likely to become helpless one day. Then she will be carried into hospital to die. She also knows that were she to be put into a nursing home at this stage of her life, she would wither in spirit and die more quickly. She cherishes her mental awareness and keeps it as keen as possible by doing crosswords, word games and keeping up her outside interests. She is experienced in knowing her needs. She is able to enjoy her memories. In her case consciousness, experience and memory have come together to enable her to live each present moment to the full, despite her very evident infirmities.

Her independent spirit should be saluted. Her stubbornness may be inconvenient to members of her family and her friends. They would be less anxious if she was safely looked after for twenty-four hours a day. It may be less efficient for local social services and caring agencies to care for her at home rather than in a purpose-built nursing home. Dilys' spirit has been enhanced by her courage and determination. Who among those who care about her would want to take that away from her? That rhetorical question might be resoundingly answered, 'No one'. Alas, she might still have to be moved. In the twenty-first century, the spiritual needs of elderly human beings are sometimes treated as if they did not exist. They do.

Dilys's story does not necessarily apply to all very old people. It does, however, challenge those who care about older people. Carers need to consider the importance of the human spirit as 'the ultimate and intimate expression' of a person's individuality. Community agencies and governments need to attend to the needs of the human spirit in all people, specially in those who are becoming dependent on other people's goodwill towards them. A caring society's concern should be to maximize the quality of people's lives rather than diminishing it by undue concern for their bodies.

No Surrender to Imprisonment of the Mind

It is probable that those who read about Dilys will immediately point out that she has retained her mental ability. What of those who do not, who suffer from a greater or lesser degree of memory loss? What can be said of those who forget that they have put the kettle on until it boils dry? They smoke cigarettes in bed, and then fall asleep. They get lost when shopping. They get up at three in the morning. Should they not be protected from the consequences of their memory loss? In extreme cases – yes, they should be. There are, however, ways of helping muddled patients to remain as independent as possible in their own homes. These ways can be tried before a decision is made to stop people living in their own homes. Those who live in familiar surroundings with familiar routines can sustain independent living. They can thrive for longer than if they are moved to new places with very different routines.

Each individual merits an individual approach, and individual solutions, to the problems that come with longevity. Take another real person, Bert.[9] Bert fought in the World War of 1939–45. Then he became a teacher. He never married, but he had a devoted niece who arranged for him to live in sheltered accommodation. By this time his short-term memory was already very poor. He had, however, developed a good routine and would go out to buy a paper at the local shop every morning. He read it with pleasure. His home help came each day. He ate her good food. He spent the long afternoon in front of the television unless someone came in to see him.

The local Alzheimer's society arranged for him to have a 'buddy'. Her role was to visit him as a friend. 'Oh, it's you', he would say; 'have a cup of tea?'

'Thank you,' came the reply. She knew that he would forget what he had offered to do almost as soon as he had said it.

The two friends would sit down and talk about their memories of the Second World War. Bert's were vivid and repetitive. He must have told the same stories a couple of hundred times during the years of his 'buddy's' visits. No other subject could engage him. They watched football and rugby on the television together and shouted hilariously when a goal was scored by either side. They never talked about anything else. Despite his trip to the newsagent each morning, Bert had lost contact with other people's 'present moments'. He wanted to live in his memories. Then he was a strong, cricket-playing young officer.

After a while, the visitor might say, 'How about that cup of tea then?' 'Oh, yes, of course,' he would say, getting up with alacrity. Five minutes later, a cup of strong black coffee would appear. Bert was a delight. He enjoyed his visits; so did his visitor.

Bert managed to stay in his own home to the end of his life. His memory got worse and worse. He no longer knew who people were, except in a very vague manner. He developed a massive tumour of his jaw. He ignored it. It grew larger and larger. One day his niece rang to say that he had died suddenly.

Happy Bert: happy those who knew him. He taught them how to live in other people's present moments rather than their own. He showed them how to extract happiness from apparent tragedy. Those skills will serve them well when they sit by someone, like him, who is content to 'tell old tales, laugh at gilded butterflies and hear poor rogues talk of court news'.[10]

It has already been pointed out in Chapter 2 that Alzheimer's disease is not always so kind. Some people know that their memories are deteriorating. They suffer greatly. Some, like Helen Waddell[11] and Iris Murdoch,[12] become frightened or aggressively frustrated. Relatives almost invariably find the destruction of the personality in someone they love very distressing. This aspect of the condition will be discussed in Chapter 5.

The freedom that comes from living in the present moment is not confined to older people, or to disabled people. Religious writers like Brother Lawrence[13] and Père de Caussade[14] have written extensively on this subject for people who are trying to live Christian lives of prayer. Their ideas are important to people of religious faith in older age, which forms part of the contents of Chapter 6.

In this century people like Nelson Mandela[15] and Archbishop Desmond Tutu[16] are outstanding examples of people who sustained their freedom during long imprisonment. Mandela spent twenty-five years as a prisoner on Robben Island. Tutu, though free, was imprisoned by apartheid. One example of their free spirits will suffice. On 29 April 2005, Archbishop Tutu was asked if he was an optimist. 'No,' he replied, 'I am a willing prisoner of hope.'[17] In this chapter the aim is to find those factors that can help many older people to live in that freedom.

The spirituality of later life is in part defined by this idea of gaining freedom through resistant acceptance. People who cannot embrace old age, and its infirmities and indignities, do not seem to be able to do very much with their later years beyond pretending to youth, or grumbling about its loss. The key to a lively old age is to accept that one is old, to embrace its unavoidable limitations and to determine to find ways round those disabilities and limitations. Spirituality is anything that helps older people to declare that their humanity is alive and well. Older people are individuals of worth. They have human rights. They still have much to contribute to their communities and society.

No Surrender: the Freedom of 'End Time'

When human beings reach very old age they know that their days are numbered. Their time on earth is limited. The present moment of *this* moment takes on a precious quality when people know that they may never see another daffodil, or a humble violet. So the sight of a daffodil or a violet is intense. It is also possible, though not always, to enjoy every contact with their relatives and friends, young and old.

Thankfulness and spiritual growth are gifts to those who live in 'end time', time that is limited. 'End time' can be time when old people continue to sow seeds in gardens, or in pots, on the window shelves of their homes. Many elderly people continue to invest interest in their children and grandchildren. They remain involved in the doings of the world around them. Some continue to buy new clothes, even when they know they have no future need of them. By doing all these things they are investing in the future. They are saying that they have a place in it, even if it will only be that they will be remembered by some. They are free to live in the present moment, in 'now', without anxiety for tomorrow. 'Now' can encompass the past, the present and the future. It can also make a lasting impact on the future of younger generations.

Spiritual freedom, once attained, is attractive. Those who meet people like Father Cyril, Dilys, Bert, Nelson Mandela and Desmond Tutu recognize that the human spirit cannot be defeated once that freedom has been claimed. These people walk free, despite being battered by disability, broken in body and mind and crushed by cruel restraints of various kinds. They have won a victory for the human spirit.

The end of a person's life is not the sum of that life. Human beings need to remember that. Helen Waddell, author of *Heloise and Abelard*, translator of beautiful medieval Latin lyrics, died on 5 March 1965. She had suffered from increasing darkness, spiritual dereliction and destruction of her personality during the last twenty years of her life. That is not what her reading public remembers. Her spirit had already won its victory and it shone through her last lecture, the W. P. Kerr lecture, given in Glasgow on 28 October 1947. One of her audience, Barbara Vere Hodge, wrote to Helen's friend and publisher, Otto Kyllmann:

> It was a triumph, and I think that everyone who sat in that crowded lecture hall will remember the wisdom and beauty of what she said. It made one glad to see how many of the young ones were there, and to feel them warm to her voice and respond to the wisdom and renewed hope she gave them. One had the conviction that something undying and eternal was being transmitted to another generation − the essence of that spirit that went with the 'young things gathered up for exile' was being conserved and passed on through the centuries.[18]

People need to look at the whole of older people's lives, not just the end points of life, when they look at someone who is old, bedridden, in pain, in mental confusion or a coma.

The next chapter looks at how relationships can help older citizens to enjoy being old. It details some ways that such relationships enhance life for both parties. It looks at some important contributions that older people make to their families, communities and societies.

4

Relationships in Later Life

The key to a successful older life
is the wisdom that comes from
the way of integration.
(Paul Tournier, *The Seasons of Life*)[1]

The focus of the last chapter was the freedom that comes from
resistant acceptance. A free spirit is one of the key qualities for a
successful old age. This chapter is mainly about relationships
and relatedness, both of which are important in old age. The
wisdom that 'comes from the way of integration' can help
human beings to relate in a number of different ways.

Paul Tournier, a twentieth-century Swiss physician, practised
holistic medicine. This meant that he treated patients as whole
persons rather than thinking of them as a collection of inter-
related mechanical organs. The quotation that heads this chapter
comes from one of his books, called *The Seasons of Life*,
published in 1964.

Integration, Wisdom and Relationship

Integration comes from intrapersonal and interpersonal relationships. Older people remember their experiences. They
relate to them. Personal memories interact with the collective
experiences of other human beings. These bear on the 'present
moments', the 'now' of anyone's life. Older people gain understanding and wisdom as they reflect on the past. Through

experience they know that the interactions between them and others have influenced them. They also know that what is happening to them now will relate to the lives of future generations. Sometimes they can project their minds into the future and see the consequences of their actions.

Wisdom begins to come from such integrated activity. Moreover, although people have finite brains, they can use the gifts of consciousness, memory and imagination to project themselves beyond this planet into the universe. Some can even reach towards a state that lies beyond time and space. Old age offers plenty of opportunity to undertake 'space–time' travel. It is relatively easy to leap into 'before time' when people are standing on the threshold of 'after time'. Many people in later life reflect on the meaning and purpose of their lives. Younger people acquire wisdom; of course they do. The point is that older people are the guardians of wisdom. That fact is not always appreciated by younger generations.

When people move into dimensions of experience that transcend verbal, pictorial and written language they gain further wisdom. During the past century and a half scientists have explored that wave/particle nature of creation. There is evidence that wave forms of energy and matter are interchangeable.[2] This evidence makes it possible to understand that energies exist that are intangible and imperceptible until they are converted into perceptible sensations.

A couple of familiar examples illustrate how waves impinge on matter. The sun's rays pass through the stratosphere into the atmosphere. Some of the rays' wavelengths lie beyond the range of human eyes, yet they nourish material life on earth. Human beings have now harnessed other wave forms of energy. Radio waves transmitted through the atmosphere from one site can be apprehended by human beings living in a distant place and time. Scientific explanations often solve former mysteries. Human beings no longer rely on supernatural explanations for natural phenomena.

Recently, science has illuminated ideas about the nature of human beings. Formerly, human beings thought themselves to be unique among animal creatures in that they can think creatively and use language. Those aspects of humanity prompted them to consider themselves to be 'superior' to members of the animal kingdom. It is now known that other animals can think and communicate in complex ways. Pioneer work by Dr Jane Goodall,[3] for instance, demonstrated that chimpanzees had individual personalities. Some of them spontaneously learnt to use simple tools fashioned from grass stems to dig out termites from their nests. They can adopt orphans and treat themselves with simple herbal remedies. There is a picture of Dr Goodall in existence that shows her communicating with a chimpanzee.[4] Other scientists have shown that some great apes can communicate in sign language.[5]

Non-verbal communication is easy to demonstrate within the human species. Spoken words sometimes convey one meaning and/or feeling: at the same time the body is expressing an opposite thought and feeling. The non-verbal communication is perceptible to the person who hears the words. Thoughts and feelings can be shared without a word being said. That is easiest when people are physically close to one another, but it can take place during telephone conversations and even through nuances in letters and emails. A current of feeling between two people, or between a person and another living being, can transcend their ability to communicate through close contact. Long-distance thinking and feeling exchanges will be discussed later in this chapter.

The reality of non-verbal exchanges may be ignored or dismissed as an inexact method of communication. Non-verbal communication *is* liable to misinterpretation. Nevertheless, it occurs and is a significant factor in relationships. It can make or break friendships, enhance or destroy companionship.

The Importance of Relationships to Older People

Regular companionship is vital to older people. It is well known that older people's lives can be revitalized by the companionship of pets, plants, or any creature to which they can relate. That relationship is enhanced if they also care for the object to which they relate. Contact that leads to real relationship is a vital ingredient of a successful old age. It is far from easy to achieve, as will be shown in the next chapter that discusses the spiritual care of older people, particularly those who are housebound. It is important to persist with efforts to help older people make relationships. People in their later years are blessed if they have relatives or friends who visit. This is specially true if visitors are willing to share thoughts and local gossip. Those who watch a programme on television with the older person, instead of turning the 'telly' on as they leave, are valuable.

It is less easy for older people to feel they have a share in the world when they are aged and housebound. This is particularly so if they have moved away from a familiar neighbourhood to sheltered, or residential, care. Older people experience real deprivation when this happens. They may sink into apathy. 'Uprooting', however necessary, or undertaken in a kindly way, is one of the greatest hazards of ageing, specially as so many sheltered accommodations and nursing homes do not welcome pets.

Even if people are uprooted, slightly confused by their new surroundings and have to form entirely new relationships, many are still able to retain control over their lives. They will insist on as much independence as possible so that they can continue to relate to the outside world. One of the residents in a sheltered accommodation complex, for instance, always goes out to buy his paper early in the morning. He is no youngster. He could easily have it delivered. Going out to buy that paper keeps him mobile. He can see other people who are also out and about at that time of the day. He might also have a brief chat in the shop. It is amazing how such small expressions of that kind of desire to relate can make such a difference to the quality of life in older people.

Close contact with other people is one of the best ways of remaining related. Older people offer invaluable help in charity shops. They study with the Open University and go to seminars. They take up some enthralling subject of study, for which they never had time when younger. In modern societies in the northern hemisphere many retired and older people can, and do, still keep in contact with what is happening in other parts of the world.

As individuals grow older, many find they can no longer relate to other people or activities for long periods of time. Younger people sometimes treat them as passive objects, but they are not. They can ask their relatives and friends for shorter visits. They may find hobbies or studies tiring; they can control the time they give to such activities. Good use can be made of quite short periods of time. An old friend, for instance, used to knit two rows at a time and then rest. She completed her scarf in a remarkably short time.

In later life, physical infirmity, and adverse circumstances of various kinds, can make close contact with living people, animals or even growing plants impossible. Hobbies or studies may become exhausting. Even then many people are still able to make contact and remain connected through more remote means. Telephones, computers, radio and television are able to bring messages from afar into a person's home. When an earthquake, volcano, tidal wave or tsunami causes devastation, people's distress is immediately apparent to the whole world. An older person, sitting by their television set, can share in that event in ways that were unknown a hundred years ago. Many older people are prompted by what they see into compassionate action.

The Benefits of Relationships in Later Life

Older people need to keep in touch. Then they can feel part of whatever is going on around them, even if they are confined to the house or find themselves wheelchair bound. Many can still listen to the radio or watch television. They need to retain some control over what they, or others, select for their interest. Leaving an older person by themselves, or, worse still, in a room full of other people with the television or radio on all day, produces boredom, not stimulation. Choices, being able to select what one wants to see, hear or read, are as important to older people as they are to those who have not yet reached that state. Otherwise, they will simply retreat into themselves and 'switch off'. They sometimes drift into dreamless sleep to avoid the cacophony of noise whose familiarity has produced mindlessness.

Relatives, friends, neighbours and carers can enliven very old people's spirits through visits and conversations. They can read to them when they are blind. They can do everything possible to help deaf people to use hearing aids and other helpful inventions. Those who suffer gross impairment of communication through Alzheimer's disease, or some other form of dementia, need contact with people who are still able to converse, and exchange positive feelings, with them.

The seventeenth-century poet, John Donne, gave insight into the human spirit when he spoke of the human condition and said, 'No man is an *Island,* entire of itself.'[6] Human beings need the 'other' to complete themselves. Isolation, loneliness and boredom are destructive to the quality of life in old people. Everything should be done to help them to accept ageing. Older people sometimes need encouragement to circumvent some of the hazards of later life.

Loneliness, Isolation and Feelings of Unrelatedness

Contact, companionships and being cared for by other people are important components of later life. Unfortunately it is possible to have all these advantages and still feel unrelated. Sadly, some older people are shunned by relatives and friends. Some older people become bitterly angry with relatives and former friends. Bitterness is a cancer of the human spirit. It is not a constructive or creative way of living one's later years. Even if people have good relationships to the end of their lives many older people still feel lonely. One of the major reasons for these negative feelings is that many older people feel they are always at the receiving end of other people's kindness or patience. They feel, rightly or wrongly, that they are always taking, and have little to give. If they do try to give to others, their contributions may not be wanted. So they begin to lose that important sense of relatedness that helps human beings to flourish. There is a longing among most human beings for real relationships, for the opportunity to share their thoughts and feelings, to make a difference to the world in which they live. Modern society is slow at recognizing the value of the wisdom of older people. Many aged people find themselves comparatively alone. They are still active enough to care for themselves. They have little or no contact with neighbours. These are the kinds of people that family doctors used to be able to visit in former times, usually once a month. Often the doctor, the milk and mail delivery persons, and the rent collector, were the only people who visited during that month.

Such individuals may feel quite unrelated to the world outside their home. They may even have given up listening to the radio, or watching television. It is hard to believe that what they do in the 'here and now' of their 'closed' environment can have any effect on creation and its inhabitants thousands of miles away, or years and years ahead. Yet, the balance of nature is held by just such positive thoughts translated into actions. The thoughts and small actions of isolated people do matter. Each major advance that benefits the world as a whole begins in one person's thought, irrespective of that person's age. Older people need to be confident. They should claim the right of any person to contribute to the thought waves that are circulating in the world. When one thought is shared by a number of people, things begin to happen. Changes come about when sufficient people share the same thought, have the capacity to express it with clarity and conviction and can persuade communities and governments to adopt those changes. However old people are, they should never stop offering their thoughts into that 'collective unconscious' of which Carl Jung spoke.[7] People become aware of their solidarity with others whenever the unconscious bursts into consciousness.

Relationships that Transcend Contact Relationships

Mention of the 'collective unconscious' again raises the difficult question as to whether or not the human spirit is an entity.

In Chapter 2, John O'Donohue defined 'spirit' as that core dimension of 'being' that brings living creatures into relationship. He suggested that the human spirit is the central dimension of personhood. It enables people to be aware of the relatedness of all creation. They do this 'through a hidden conversation between consciousness, experience and memory'.[8] Animals may have this consciousness of relatedness: human beings, having such highly complex brains, have it more than most living creatures. They can transmit it across time and space through pictorial and linguistic language.

There is another major question about human relationships. Is it possible for human beings to communicate and relate at a distance without intermediary agents like radio, television and emails? Can they do this simply through the energies called thoughts and feelings? Some people scoff at the idea. Others, including some scientists who study paranormal phenomena,[9] think that some human beings can communicate in this way. Research into telepathy, mind reading and other paranormal phenomena continues. No definite answers exist. Telepathy and paranormal powers may exist only in the imagination. Imagination is a potent creative energy. Children will play with, and talk to, imaginary playmates that they have conjured up in their minds. They talk to plants. They hear animals talking to them. They relate to imaginary children as if they were real. Some adults retain this quality of relating imaginatively. They sometimes produce great works of art, literature and music as a rich legacy to future generations.

Old people, with much acquired consciousness, experience and memory, can wander all round the world in their minds, mental imagination and dreams. They do not necessarily express these experiences and memories in outward ways, but their awareness of events in faraway places is very real. They can sometimes plumb into the 'collective unconsciousness' and make their impact on creation in that way. In doing this they acquire 'wisdom that comes from the way of integration', as Tournier says. Human spirits can find fulfilment. That richness may then become available to other people, past, present and future. Some Christians and members of other religious faiths might call this kind of relating 'prayer'. Humanists and others might refer to such communication as a mystery that cannot yet be explained scientifically. This is an area of human experience that should be taken seriously even if one is a confirmed sceptic. It is important to listen to people, specially those with proven wisdom. A life-changing encounter between the author and an older woman near the end of her life illustrates this point.

Iulia de Beausobre was well known in Christian circles. In 1938 she had published an account of her life in Russia during, and after, the Revolution of 1917. It was called *The Woman Who Could Not Die*.[10] Later, she had published a book called *Creative Suffering*.[11] She wrote it during the 1939–45 World War. It detailed her reflections on the nature of suffering at the hands of other human beings. It was also partly about her experience of imprisonment in Russia. While she was in prison her husband was shot by Communists. Her baby son starved to death. The book impressed and helped many people during those war years. Meeting her was an opportunity to express gratitude for her writing.

Iulia was a slender, upright old lady with white hair. She sat straight backed in an armchair in the small, rather bare room that was her home. She had also written a biographical account of her relationship with her second husband, the economist, Lewis Namier.[12] Constance Babbington-Smith had written her biography.[13]

Such a person commanded respect. Her answer to a question about what she was doing with her time was, however, startling: 'Scouring the world with my dead skin, mopping up the evil in it,' she said. Her answer was incomprehensible at the time. It was not until much later that her cryptic remark began to make some sense.

Iulia was trying to speak about the way she thought the core of her personality, her human spirit, permeated the whole of her being, including every cell of her body. She knew that human bodies shed surface skin cells every day. She had come to the conclusion that her life and those cells had some continuity. Iulia thought this meant that when skin cells fell off her body they became part of the dust of the earth, blown into the wind, or buried in a compost heap somewhere. Each cell would contain something of her spirit. This spirit would clean up the evil that she met with through her relatedness to creation.

Iulia's thoughts startled her visitor. Until she met Iulia the visitor had rather thought of the human spirit as that which connected the 'soul', a distinct entity separate from the body, to God. Iulia, however, did not think like that at all. She thought of the human spirit as being in every cell of her body. She saw dying as a continual fact of every life. Every day she was reaching out into the atmosphere through her dead skin cells. In her mind they were still connected to her living cells through her human spirit, the core of her personality.

The meeting provoked all sorts of questions. What happens to the human spirit when an arm or leg is amputated and its still living cells are cut off from the rest of the body? What happens to another person's spirit when someone receives a transplanted heart? What happens to human spirits when people's bodies die and decompose? These and other such questions have been raised since the date of that meeting. They may seem ridiculous to scientists, but they are questions that family doctors will sometimes hear voiced when transplant surgery is being discussed. At the time Iulia's ideas provoked scepticism, yet hindsight enabled a deeper reflection on her statement, and a better understanding of some patients' hesitations about transplant surgery.

The ideas of older people should not be discounted quickly. They merit thought. There are no answers that fully satisfy a person's rational self. They compel thought every time that people talk about 'our bodies, souls and spirits' as if they were separate entities jostling for attention. Human bodies are always changing in their composition. Cells are being created throughout life. They are also dying. The composition of a person's body changes completely during life. Is the person who was born the same person as the one who dies? That question brings more conundrums that beg for answers. If the human spirit is an essential part of the personality what becomes of it after death? Religious people from all faiths may provide some answers to those sorts of questions. Often, however, the answers do not satisfy a searching mind, especially in later life, when an individual becomes aware of the closeness of the impending death of vital organs.

This sort of question that comes out of a relationship with an older person, like Iulia de Beausobre, can be very enriching. It gives the older person an opportunity to communicate. It gives the listener an opportunity to think hard.

Paradoxically, however, more people seem able to learn from the expressed wisdom of fictional characters. These regularly appear in modern fantasy tales, myths, film, television and computer images. These fictional characters convey something of the possibility of integration and harmonious relationships in the characters they portray. Characters like Gandalf and Galadriel in J.R.R. Tolkein's *Lord of the Rings*,[14] Obi-Wan Kenobi in *Star Wars*[15] and Professor Dumbledore[16] in the Harry Potter books and films are warmly appreciated. Younger people seem to find it harder to profit from the wisdom of real old persons. This may be because such encounters are often challenging. The following account of an ordinary pastoral visit, very different from that of the author's meeting with Iulia de Beausobre, illustrates this point

A priest used to visit one of his very old parishioners. The old man and the priest enjoyed chatting about old times. They gossiped about things of mutual interest. During each visit 'Tom' challenged the priest with an awkward question about his faith. Together they would struggle to find answers. Only rarely were there answers that could satisfy both. 'Tom's' wisdom in continuing to wrestle with the great issues of human life was teaching his younger visitor to go on learning, exploring, wrestling, being willing to change opinions as he became older himself.

Iulia's and 'Tom's' stories are central to this chapter. They underlie one of the reasons for writing a book about the spirituality that is a feature of older age. It is to encourage people who are not yet older, or who are in the early stages of later life, to learn from those who are older something of a particular way of integration that brings fulfilment.

The Wisdom of Older People that Comes from Relatedness

Wisdom comes from older people who have learnt the way of resistant acceptance and who are able to integrate experiences. It also comes from those who become acutely aware of relatedness in their old age.

In later life, many people acquire the 'wisdom that comes from the way of integration'. They gather the past, present and future into the present moment. That wisdom can be available to all people, of all faiths and none. It would seem sensible for younger people in industrialized societies to take the time and trouble to ask older people for their views. In this way they tap the wisdom beyond understanding. One seemingly obscure thought can provoke a response that may subsequently affect the future of humankind. The 'now' of such encounters may form part of their and our futures.

It is not easy to enter into older people's present moments. Those who are younger can help older people to feel valuable by encouraging their memories. The residents of one sheltered home, for instance, sometimes talk about the wartime days. Some of them are as much as twenty years older than the youngest of them, but all are old enough to have lived through those five years. Telling stories to one another brings the past into the present. The stories bring bitter memories, but also memories of kindness and compassion from wartime comrades. Engaging in such conversations can bring an awareness that human spirits are reaching out to each other's past. Then, suddenly, people find themselves sharing in a present experience of communal thoughts and feelings. They find themselves relating to one another as equal partners in life. In some mysterious way, past and present have become an integral part of that solidarity of being human persons joined together by communal experiences and memories.

The Role of Carers in Making Interpersonal Relationships with Older People

Those who care for older people have responsibility. They can help people in later life to remember. They can listen to 'old tales', repeatedly. They can look at photographs. They can sing old songs and hymns that are familiar to older people. Such activities are *not* just a way of pleasing old people; nor are they patronizing unless that attitude is conveyed through non-verbal language. Such activities are life-giving for old people, even if some of the stories have grown a bit unreal with repetitive telling. Some are distorted by rose-coloured memories. These activities are also life-giving for younger people. Older people need to find the courage to talk about their lives to younger people. That is one of the ways that they will have a part in the future of their families, friends and colleagues.

Carers should also encourage people in later life to resist isolation. Too often, for all sorts of reasons, older people drop out of the sight of the communities of which they had once been an important part. 'Out of sight, out of mind' leads to separation, isolation and loss of interrelatedness between different generations. It results in the loss of human wisdom. The whole community loses an inherent part of itself. Hospitals and old people's homes become dumping places for lonely old people. There never seems to be enough time for professional carers to listen, or learn, from the people entrusted to them. Things have gone badly wrong in societies that seek to shut old people into segregated areas that, though comfortable enough, do not enhance the human spirit in any real way.

Carers can also encourage older people to seek reconciliation with former enemies, even if those enemies are long-standing. This aspect of unhappy relationships in later life is all too real in some people's lives and can destroy a person's peace of mind at the end of life.

Society's Responsibility Towards Older People

Citizens of a materialistic, consumerist, technological society are in danger of losing any appreciation of the worth of older people. This is shown by the way that society treats pensioners. Older people are often treated as if they always need help and assistance. They are usually regarded as frail in body and mind. They are seldom approached as sources of wisdom from which the young can learn. Recent evidence shows that sometimes old people are denied drugs that could help them because of their age.[17] Such 'ageism' is an ugly feature of postmodern society.

Some of these issues will be raised again in later chapters. Meanwhile it seems good to continue to explore ways in which the sun can shine at the sunset of people's lives. It is true that many people miss the sunshine of later life because they feel frustrated. This often happens because it is easier to relate to past experience. It is sometimes more satisfying to compare the present with the past in unfavourable and highly critical ways. 'Looking back' may influence their present perspective on life. It may prevent them from seeing what is good about the present, and what might be better if they allowed themselves to contribute to the future.

Currently, many people of all ages are looking for a satisfactory spirituality that will nourish them. Society as a whole needs to recognize the worth of old people. Much of what young people now know has come from living with, caring for and learning from older people Older people who accept their age, yet resist its ravages, can be inspiring. Those who are determined to relate to the whole of creation, and within that creation to relate to themselves in creative ways, have much to offer to younger people. If young people can build on those strengths their spirits will thrive.

Older people often know what they want. They have learnt from others. They know what will nourish human spirits. They have much to give to those who can receive their wisdom. They are the people who, more than most, have good ideas about their needs. Principal among those needs is the need for a dignified old age among people to whom they can relate creatively. These should be the main concerns of those who try to care humanely for them towards the end of their lives.

5

Caring for the Human Spirit of Older People

On Monday when the sun is hot
I wonder to myself a lot:
'Now is it true, or is it not,
That what is which and which is what?'
(A. A. Milne, *Winnie-the-Pooh*, 1892–1956)[1]

For all knowledge and wonder (which is the seed of knowledge) is an impression of pleasure in itself.
(Francis Bacon, *Advancement of Learning*, 1561–1626)[2]

Valid issues were raised in the last chapter about the existence, nature and location of the human spirit. They deserve serious consideration. They invite decision. On balance, this writer prefers to affirm the existence and individuality of the human spirit than to deny it. John O'Donohue's statement in Chapter 2 seems a good working definition. He states that the human spirit is 'the source from which consciousness, experience and memory unfold and the place to which they gather and return.'[3] So those who care for the human spirit in old age should give priority to the care of human consciousness, experience and memory. One way in which these faculties of the brain relate to each other is through the experience that is called 'wonder'. Before looking at wonder, however, it is necessary to look at how consciousness, experience and memory relate in the brain.

Brain Function in Conscious and Unconscious People

Human beings at any age, providing they have well-functioning brains, can think, ask questions, make discoveries, learn, feel and relate. It used to be thought that these activities were restricted to human beings. In the twenty-first century, however, the work of primatologists, such as Jane Goodall, Dian Fossey and Biruté Galdikas,[4] has shown that some animals can communicate, even across species, learn and make discoveries. It is also known that human beings and chimpanzees share 99.4 per cent of their DNA.[5] Curiosity and thinking are well-established facts among primates. Emotions are present in apes, although awe has not, as far as is known by this author, been the subject of detailed investigation. If it is present, then human beings have this quality in greater measure.

Human solidarity with the animal kingdom also has been demonstrated by some meticulous twentieth-century research. It was undertaken by Professor Adrian of Cambridge University. He showed that 'the same kind of activity is found in all sorts of nerve fibres from all sorts of animals and there is no evidence to suggest that any other kind of activity is possible'.[6] So animals and human beings are now known to have far more in common than was once thought.

Further facts are beginning to emerge about the function of the brain during consciousness and unconsciousness. The pioneering work done by Dr David Menon at Addenbrooke's Hospital trauma unit on comatose patients has already been mentioned in Chapter 2. Such work on the unconscious brain is still in its early stages. It implies that under certain circumstances the unconscious brain can remember. Menon's findings, if proved and extended by further research, have consequences for old people who are not fully conscious, or who are in a 'vegetative state'.[7] They will be discussed again in Chapter 8.

Some scientists have suggested that when a specific part of the human brain is stimulated it produces feelings associated with religious faith.[8] This may suggest to some people that faith is a function of the brain. To others it suggests that the brain has a receptor area that responds to the reality of God.

These findings suggest that animal brains and human brains are highly complex organs. Identical electronic impulses connect different parts of the brain – the cerebral hemispheres, the cerebellum, the hypothalamus and limbic systems and the brain stem. Yet the consequences are different.

Wonder may simply be a function of the human brain. If that is so it must be admitted that the human brain is remarkably capable of producing it so as to provide people with a sense of the transcendent, a knowledge, or 'knowing', that goes beyond the limits of experience and understanding. People of religious faith may dissent from the idea that wonder is an experience that originates solely in the human brain. They would want to say that wonder is the result of an interaction between the human person and another distinct agency. They commonly name this other agency as God.

Wonder that Comes from Consciousness, Experience and Memory

In the previous section of this chapter, the author stated that she has not yet been able to find any research on the sense of wonder or 'awe' in animals. That does not preclude its existence. The experience of wonder does, however, exist among human beings.

There are at least three kinds of wonder. There is the kind of 'wonder' that comes from thinking that leads to curiosity. That, presumably, is the kind that Winnie the Pooh indulges in on Mondays, and that Francis Bacon thinks of as 'the seed of knowledge'. Curiosity leads to knowledge. In the quotation from Bacon, however, the word may have had a second meaning for the author. He uses 'wonder' as 'the seed of knowledge' but then links it to pleasure. The second kind of 'wonder' includes an element of surprise that comes out of curiosity. This sudden realization of a fact one was previously unaware of is called an 'ah ha' experience, the sort Isaac

Newton experienced on seeing an apple fall from a tree. The third kind of 'wonder' is the focus for this chapter. It is the sense of reverent awe that emerges from a sequence of events. Curiosity leads to knowledge; knowledge combined with feeling leads to a sense of reverent awe. Our forebears, especially those who wrote prayers and hymns, used 'wonder' and 'awe' easily and frequently. Both words describe the reverent astonishment that is the result of thinking in a way that combines thought and curiosity with feeling. The seventeenth-century poet and writer, Joseph Addison (1672–1713), wrote about wonder in this way. In the opening verse of one of his hymns he says:

> When all thy mercies, O my God,
> my rising soul surveys,
> transported with the view, I'm lost
> in wonder, love and praise.[9]

Wonder is not, however, necessarily associated with any religious faith: all human beings can experience wonder. It is the way the human spirit expresses itself when it discovers relatedness in a new and mysterious way. The next section of this chapter is concerned with finding ways to help older people to retain and develop their sense of wonder.

Wonder is a vital ingredient of human life. Spirituality should foster wonder at any age. So the care of the human spirit in older people must include the retention and development of wonder in all of its three senses.

The Care of the Human Spirit: Fostering Wonder

Much of the care of the human spirit in later life necessarily depends on older people themselves. Bodily states are important; well-being, disability and ill health all impinge on human spirits. In this chapter, however, the focus is on ways of preserving and developing human capacity for wonder that make full use of consciousness, experience and memory.

It is not enough to keep people's minds active in later life.

Carers can, and often do, encourage older people to study, create works of art, relate and remain involved in some way with local and world affairs. Individuals can do all these things and still remain seriously undernourished in spirit. They will starve if they do not experience curiosity, surprise, amazement, wonder and reverent awe. These transcend the immediate perceptions of conscious thinking and feeling.

The importance of wonder in all three of its meanings was revealed by a friend, 'Alice', who was immobilized by a disabling illness. It kept her housebound for several weeks. Relatives, friends and the local medical and social services rallied to her help. She had moderately severe high frequency hearing impairment and tinnitus, so music and the spoken word no longer gave her as much pleasure as they once did. So she immersed herself in reading, knitting and study with the Open University. These activities satisfied her curiosity, creativity and knowledge. They did awaken a sense of wonder at times. Yet, she found that she was missing a vital ingredient of her former existence. She missed the beauty that lay out of sight out of doors. She missed her daily walks.

'Alice' said that when she became aware of her lack she began to think about other things that she had missed since becoming older, more disabled and less able to travel independently. Formerly, she had not recognized her loss. Now, she missed being able to choose her own books at the library. She felt bereft at the loss of her visits to museums, theatres and cinemas. There she had seen pictures, plays and films that stimulated her need for transcendence. Her home contains some beautiful things. It is full of growing plants and books. There is, however, a limit to the number of plants that can be grown on the windowsills of a relatively small flat. Some of her books about art are now too heavy for her to manage comfortably. Most of all, she found that she was hesitant to impose her needs on other people who 'came by'. Visitors were solicitous, but had little time for the kinds of prolonged encounters that can evoke a shared sense of wonder.

This experience of the loss of mobility and independence

suggests that it is relatively easy for individuals to become insensitive to wonder. Once aware of that lack, older people need to make an effort to find the beauty they are missing. They can find it in memories of experiences. They can recall physical beauty through, for instance, looking at photographs of places they had once visited. People like 'Alice' may explore nuances of meaning in words. They may begin to notice beauty in their limited environments and in their daily contacts. They may begin to look for the minute, invisible structures that exist in material objects. In these ways they can recover their sense of wonder. They can also realize that they can cultivate a sense of wonderment by asking the kind of questions that Winnie the Pooh asked, and that are to be found in Francis Bacon's aphorism.

This story had a happy ending. It helped one person to learn that she had to be positive about seeking wonder. From that time onwards she took any opportunities she could to find wonder inside herself, in her environment and in her relationships with the created world in which she lives. When she recovered, she went out into the park on her own for the first time. She experienced the vividness of its natural beauty. It brought her near to ecstasy. This experience taught her to hold on to whatever choices she could make to foster a sense of wonder. She learnt to ask for what she needed to preserve that sense of the transcendent.

Caring for the Human Spirit: Asking for Help to Preserve a Sense of Wonder

Life before retirement, before increasing physical disabilities, before needing to admit that one is old, contains abundant opportunities for wonder. Older people have to accept their current limitations. These limitations need not make inroads on the quality of wonder that the human spirit positively needs.

Older people sometimes find it very hard to know what they need. Even when they do know, they find it harder still to ask for help to get what they need to flourish in old age. They are used to finding their way round their disabilities. They have learnt to go beyond them. Inevitably, however, the approach of very old age means that, at some time or another, they will need to ask for help to get what they need. Older people need to practise asking for help in a confident way, both in their younger days and in very old age.

People who belong to the older generation often find it hard to ask for what they need. They do not want to bother other people. They pride themselves on their independence. They may be afraid of becoming a nuisance. They are often afraid of rejection. These inner feelings may seem ridiculous to those who care about, and for, elderly people. They are, however, common among people who are dependent on others. If older people are too proud, or too nervous, to ask for what they need to nourish their human spirits, they will wither. It is helpful if younger people sense this need for wonder in those for whom they care.

Caring for the Human Spirit: Offering Help to Preserve a Sense of Wonder

Those who try to care for older people are often quite skilled about providing for their basic bodily and emotional needs. They are sometimes less skilled in caring for an elderly person's questing spirit. Many older people are curious, and want to go on asking important questions about 'what is which and which is what?' They need to contemplate the meaning and purpose of their lives. They continue to search for answers to the great questions about the beginnings and endings of life as they have known it during their lifetimes. Many people need to acquire knowledge. Most of all, perhaps, they need to preserve their sense of reverent awe.

Now carers are sometimes even less skilled at knowing how to engender wonder and a sense of the mysteries of life, a 'knowing'. Those skills are intuitive and transcend understanding. Ministers of faith should be the most likely people to foster transcendence and wonder among older people. They have a prime responsibility for the human spirit, the core element of personality that enables people to relate. The next chapter of this book will examine some of the positive ways in which ministers of faiths and caring people can assist older people to foster a sense of reverence and awe. At this point, however, there is need to mourn the loss of wonder that seems to have overcome many churches and religious institutions today. This degree of criticism should not deter anyone from continuing to search for wonder. Perhaps some ministers of religion may take note?

Thomas Carlyle (1795–1881) once described worship as 'transcendent wonder'.[10] The use of clumsy language and ritual deters many people from participating in opportunities for wonder. Unfortunately, many modern worship services abound in a multitude of words. Many of these words are made unintelligible by poor diction and poorer sound systems. Many services lack silence. Many services are too long. All these factors make it harder for ageing bodies to endure discomforts of all kinds. They may decide to stay at home. Quite quickly they lose touch with the faith community.

In one sense, none of that loss of the numinous dimension of worship should stop any old person from seeking wonder. Individuals can help themselves to achieve a sense of wonder wherever they are. All people have to do is to know their need and look actively for it wherever they can find it. Wonder can pour into people's lives through music, art, drama, touch, intimacy. They can experience warm silence and the shared emotion of sorrow or delight at any time of life. Wonder is most needed, perhaps, when men and women are on the threshold of the completion of their lives. Such moments of wonder can come to them from sensitive relatives, friends and all sorts of relationships.

Older people should not be afraid to ask for help. They should ask to be taken out. They should not be ashamed to be wheeled along to an art exhibition. They can and should ask for discussion on matters that really concern them. Many of them would positively welcome the opportunity to talk about their past lives, their present ones and the approaching fact of dying and death. Some older people talk to themselves, to the walls of their homes, to plants, to the sky. They will often talk to pets, children, passers-by, anyone who is intuitive to their needs. They should not be afraid to ask to be touched lovingly, even kissed. Intimate moments of shared wonder are among the most precious experiences in life.

Similarly, those who care for people in later life should not be afraid to offer such help to those who may be too shy to ask for what they need. Carers can be aware of unspoken anxieties about life and death issues. They can gently initiate discussions that may be painful, but that may also relieve anxiety. One thing is sure. Shared intimacy among human beings can heighten the sense of wonder in one or more of the individuals who experience it.

It is not enough for younger people, who care for, and about, older people, to 'pass the buck', to recommend someone else to attend to the spiritual needs of older people. Being satisfied that one has done one's best by sending for the nearest clergy person, or minister of faith, to talk to an older person is a way of 'opting out' of a painful fact. The human spirit needs intuitive under-standing, amounting to empathy, from at least one other human spirit, preferably more, to attain to that 'peace that passes all understanding'. That peace comes from an experience of tran-scendence and awe. Empathy needs to be more available to older people than it can be from the occasional visit of an 'expert'. 'Experts' are not always attuned to the needs of the human spirit.

There are many ways into an older person's needs. They need touches of love. They need people who sense anxieties before they are voiced. They delight in shared experiences and memories. They also need people to listen to them. When an older person shares the fruits of wisdom with a younger person, they can share moments of intimate understanding, apprehen-sion of mystery and wonder. Those experiences can lead to a sense of fulfilment that is as precious to older people as it is to the younger generation. As has already been noted, a sense of wonder is a precious gift in later life. It may stand individuals in good stead if, and when, they are assaulted by some of the difficulties of later life.

Anxiety that Interferes with the Well-being of the Human Spirit in Older People

Certain factors in human personality, experience and memory can interfere with the health of the human spirit in later life. One of these is undue anxiety. Older people often experience severe anxiety over relatively minor matters. They may find themselves increasingly worried when they forget other people's names. They feel distressed when they are unable to remember where their missing keys are. They dither about whether it is safe to go out of the house alone at night. They may feel troubled about a careless word they have spoken. They may just feel 'fussed' because things have not gone the way they hoped they would. Sometimes, especially after an accident or a debilitating illness, even the most well-organized and least anxious of people finds it hard to regain confidence and independence. This sense of 'whirling anxiety' that goes on inside some people's heads can spoil their pleasure in life. It makes it very difficult, if not impossible, to feel at peace, to be content, happy, joyful about themselves and their circumstances. This is where they can help themselves, and be helped.

Strategies for Managing Anxiety

'It doesn't matter,' a loving daughter-in-law says to her mother-in-law when the old lady is agitated about having broken, or lost, something. 'Just sit down and get your breath, while I look around.' The old woman sits down. She feels foolish. The keys are being searched for, or the broken bits of china are being swept into a dustpan. She is far from calm at this moment. She is faced with choice. She can admit that at this present moment she is fussed, or she must vehemently deny it. If she realizes that she is agitated and cannot be calm, she may be able to laugh gently to herself. If she does that, she may become thankful for the opportunity to catch her breath.

Laughter is a wonderful antidote to anxieties. It needs to be cultivated. Reading jokes and funny stories to oneself, or to older friends and relatives, is not a trivial activity at all. There is, for instance, a well-known Jewish joke about a man who fell off a cliff. On his way down he clutches at the slender trunk of a little tree growing out of the cliff side. He realizes the tree is not going to hold him for long. He is not a person of religious faith. However, in his extremity he prays to God: 'If there's anyone up there,' he says, 'do something to help me.' A comforting voice replies. 'Don't worry; I'll hold you up. Just let go and trust in my strong arms underneath you.' The man is surprised. He did not expect any answer. He thinks for a long time. The tree begins to shake. He calls out: 'Is there anyone else up there?'

Poor man. He might have trusted a human voice. Quite probably a human being was not anywhere near at hand. God might, or might not, have saved his physical life. He could not be confident enough to let go and trust there was a God who would allow him to fall to his death, yet save him in a different way. Rabbi Lionel Blue, who once told this story in a slightly different version, commented:

> Humour is one way, and not the least important by which we come to consider the cosmos in which we live – with its treasures, paradoxes, absurdities, heights, despairs and depths, its love, irony, brutality and hidden laughter.[11]

Watching comedy on television provides a time of escape from the harsh realities of old age. In Britain there was a remarkably successful comedy programme about a curmudgeonly old man and his long suffering wife.[12] Many of his adventures were the result of human frailty in older age. To laugh at them was to laugh gently at oneself. Sometimes the viewers could distance themselves from what was happening. Sometimes they could identify with the various characters in the programme. Either way, laughter of that kind is healing.

One of the best ways of using kindly laughter is in the company of relatives or old friends. Being able to raise comic memories of past events in one's life can be a shared pleasure. It abates anxiety, even fear, even minor guilt. It will not abate clinical depression, and may increase it. Unkind laughter, laughter at someone's expense, is never justified and can do harm.

Tears also are a gift. 'If I didn't laugh, I'd cry' is a comment that is frequently made after a good session of laughter. Laughter and tears *are* closely linked. Older people – indeed human beings of any age – should never be ashamed to cry. It is often healthy to cry. The unspoken sorrows of life can sometimes be assuaged by reading a sad story or watching a 'weepy movie'. Paradoxically, beauty or a newborn child can move people to tears of joy. Both are healthy expressions of natural emotions.

Carers need to understand that tears in older age are natural. They sometimes need expression rather than instant comfort. Being able to cry in the presence of a relative, friend or sympathetic carer releases pent-up emotions that can do harm to the human spirit. Sensitive carers will just sit and let the tears flow. That is more immediately important than over hasty discernment of the cause of the tears. Later on, the older person may be able to talk about the cause of their overflowing emotions.

Healthy laughter and tears need to be distinguished from pathological conditions that amount to sickness. Some disturbances of the brain can affect centres in the brain that control laughter and crying. Such laughter is inconsequential. It often occurs without any outer stimulus at all. This kind of laughter and tears can afflict an older person after a 'stroke'. There is no emotion involved. It just happens. Again, carers need to deal with those kind of laugher and tears calmly. If they get distressed, the older person will become so too. If they remain calm, the episode will quickly pass. This is where skilled and sensitive professional help can do so much to reassure both carers and those for whom they care. Pathological crying may also accompany depression and guilt. These conditions are examined later in this chapter.

There are other ways of dealing with anxieties that come from human frailty, as described in the older woman who lost her keys. If she has had much practice, she can distract herself from anxiety by moving her mind somewhere more peaceful and happy. This strategy works well for some older people. From time to time, close friends may need to remind their older friends about this. One older person does this for herself. There are three pictures in her living room. From her usual chair she can see all of them at the same time. Each is of a place or person she has known and loved, where she has found happiness and peace. Whenever she feels unduly anxious she looks at one of them, or, indeed, at all of them. She can then recapture the pleasurable moment she once experienced. She can allow it to overlap the unpleasant immediate moment. That recalled memory can often transform a difficult situation.

Some older people's anxieties come from more serious reasons like slowness of movement, sudden attacks of dizziness, 'any time of the day' tiredness and napping. Anxiety accompanies the loss of sphincter control that leads to incontinence and breaking wind. Embarrassment and a sense of lost dignity may force older people to retire into their own homes, and to seem unsociable. These people feel out of control, and/or foolish, in the sight of others. Their self-confidence may be destroyed. They may become unable to think or to discover wonder. Such anxieties need to be recognized, owned and dealt with at a practical level with sensitivity. Relatives and friends who understand why old people stay away from long meetings are precious. Friends who are aware of why old people hesitate to accept overnight invitations to friends' homes produce great relief. Such friends can sometimes enable older people to confide in them and help them to feel secure in their company.

Guilt and Depression that Interfere with the Well-being of the Human Spirit in Later Life

A more serious cause of distress comes from guilt about events of the past, or failures in relationships. The problems come from unhealed episodes in a person's life. Sometimes older people find themselves unable to forgive. Sometimes they are not forgiven. Sometimes they cannot forgive themselves. A fairly large number of older people suffer from episodes of depression that have nothing to do with actual guilt. Their brain chemistry goes wrong. They may feel guilty, but there is no substance to that guilt.

Whatever the cause, depression can virtually destroy happiness in later life. Depressed people slow down, sometimes to the point of apathy. Their appetites for pleasure of any kind, specially food, disappear. They often lose weight. Paradoxically, some overeat to compensate. They will grow obese. They no longer care about their appearance. Their sleep pattern is disturbed. They commonly say they no longer have any reason to live. They want to die. Those around them who are unaware of the malignancy of depression in later life, and that it is curable, may think the older person is asking to be put to death. This problem will be looked at again in Chapter 8.

Loneliness may aggravate depression especially if it gets a good hold and there is no one to help. Personal experience, and the experience of helping many other people during very old age and dying, suggests that an important part of every old person's living in the sunset years of life should be to find the courage to revisit and deal with past memories.

Dealing with sad memories may be hard, often is hard, but it is a worthwhile activity. It sometimes enables people to be reconciled to the past. They may then be able to leave a positive legacy of knowledge, 'wonder, love and praise' to those who will remain alive after their death. Old age is a great gift in that respect. It is one that is not always given to those who die young, unexpectedly, or who have no sense of the wonder that comes from being part of humanity.

When individuals are older, tired, fragile and lonely, sometimes feeling excluded and even unwanted, it is easy to brood over failures from the past. Such feelings always need attention. Sometimes relief may come from a reconnection with an 'old enemy', a person whom one once hurt quite a lot, or a person whose friendship was unaccountably lost. Small actions can produce remarkable effects. Older people may worry about past pique which stopped them from exchanging Christmas cards with certain friends. If they decide to send a brief note to a neglected friend it can have a remarkable effect. Such an action, even without a reply, can ease an elderly person's mind. It can help such a person feel at peace. He or she may, perhaps, find the reward of more happy memories of those past relationships. It is equally easy to brood over resentments at past hurts one has endured at the hands of others, or over misfortunes in life.

Pastoral experience over many decades suggests that depression in old age is a very serious matter. An example, such as that cited in the previous paragraph, may appear to be trivial. It seldom is trivial. It covers up more serious issues. Unhappy thoughts about broken relationships with children, ex-partners, friends, often surface in very old age. Often they are not disclosed because of shame or a feeling of hopelessness. That is where older people can benefit from help from others.

Strategies for Dealing with Guilt and Depression

Other people often know friends better than those friends know themselves. They may know their friends intuitively. Alternatively, the older person may make his or her emotional state evident without being able to say what is wrong. Small acts of kindness, such as having an unnecessary cup of tea with an older friend who seems 'a bit down', can lead to the unfolding of the cause of the misery. Telling the story may relieve considerable distress.

Clinical depression is elusive in older people. Both the older person and the carer may attribute feelings of depression to natural old age when they are not. When in doubt it is sensible to look for the signs of unusual weight loss or gain, sleep disturbance, apathy and loss of interests that were formerly present. All those symptoms call for medical diagnosis to exclude the sickness of clinical depression. Depression that has an external cause can be removed when the cause is dealt with properly. Clinical depression continues.

Guilt and anxiety that have an external cause often result in a loss of self-confidence. That loss can damage a person's ability to think, relate and develop a sense of awe. Older people are often faced with having to use a walking stick. They need magnifying glasses to complement their spectacles. They may need to lip-read even though they have good digital hearing aids. They may not be able to go out of doors without being well padded up to avoid embarrassing incontinence. So it is not surprising that they may lose confidence in themselves.

Other people's attitudes can add to an older person's loss of confidence. Sometimes, well-meaning relatives and friends are excessively anxious. They do not want those older people to fall over, or exert themselves too much. They try to stop older people from doing anything risky. Unfortunately, relatives who are *too* anxious can increase a person's loss of confidence. People who lose their self-confidence may become unable to do anything they want to do, or need to do, to foster the well-being of their human spirits. Sometimes excessive anxiety provokes a different reaction. The old person is so irritated that he or she acts hastily and irresponsibly.

Angers that Interfere with the Human Spirit in Later Life

Frustration, irritability and immoderate anger have already been mentioned in Chapter 2 of this book and they will be referred to again in Chapter 8 on Ageism. This is because these emotions are such frequent companions of old age. They affect the human spirit disproportionately. They distress carers. They may have grave consequences for the old person.

As already mentioned, some irritability is almost inevitable in the later years of life. Most of the frustration and irritability come from increasing physical and mental weakness. Many older people remember times when they were younger, more pleasant, even placid individuals. They are seriously distressed when in later years they find themselves immoderately angry over quite little things. Frustration needs an outlet. Anger is one way of dealing with that frustration. Shouting at the television, or at 'God', is one way of venting that kind of anger. It does no harm. It is much better than being unkind to a relative or friend.

Some anger, however, is not at all benign. Older people can get so angry that they do damage to things they care about, or to people they love. They may also harm themselves. This happens more often in people whose brains are damaged in some way by disease, or who are mentally ill. A formerly loving husband or wife can batter a spouse physically or emotionally. They can use what small power they have left to destroy other people's lives by cruel speech, by unjustified reproach, by 'cutting someone', even by altering their wills. It is not always easy to know where the line is between nastiness and pathological anger. Often it is a matter of degree. Often professional help is needed before discernment can be made.

One frequent scenario for immoderate anger of this pathological kind comes from an older person's move into an unfamiliar situation like a nursing home. They do not want to go. That is natural. They resent being made to go. That, too, is natural. They cannot see why they cannot be cared for at home, or in sheltered accommodation. That indicates they are no longer thinking rationally. They stubbornly dig their heels in. That indicates they are no longer able to think of other people's emotions. When eventually they do move, these resentments increase and may overflow into angry behaviour or impossible demands.

Removal from familiar surroundings and neighbours often precipitates confusion about the new situation. Confusion, resentment and anger commonly surface. Anger is directed towards the carers in the new situation. Professional carers are often patient and understanding in such situations. In time, older people generally adjust and settle down happily. Sometimes they do not. They continue to complain vigorously about their new homes. They stir up trouble among other residents. Sometimes old repressed angers surface in very unpleasant ways of accusation and suspicion. In extreme cases, relatives will be asked to remove the resident. In these situations no one is a winner, least of all the angry old person.

Another very unhappy consequence of old age, irritability, immoderate anger and unsociable attitudes is that older people sometimes begin to alienate those who love them or care for them. In some cases, carers become persecutors, or purveyors of cruelty. In extreme cases, usually among those who have to cope day in and day out with people with Alzheimer's disease, or other forms of dementia, the carers batter patients. Separation of old people from those who care for them may be the only solution in some unhappy situations.

Strategies for Dealing with Anger

Anger can be destructive to the human spirit. It sometimes turns inwards and leads to excessive guilt, depression, even to fear of damnation. It nearly always needs to be dealt with in constructive ways.

Anger needs to be expressed, preferably in a creative way. Older people swear, sometimes for the first time in their lives. They thump their sticks. They pummel cushions. They hurl abuse at 'God'. None of this does much harm and sometimes it is sufficient to dispel unpleasant moods.

Spitefulness is a different matter. It is a way of revenge. Some older people kick the cat, or take pleasure in stamping on small living creatures like ants. Often angry people hurt loving relatives and friends. If older people find themselves doing such acts of cruelty, they should realize that something is wrong. They need to find healthier ways of dealing with their anger.

Anger is best dealt with through creative activity that uses up the energy of anger. Painting, modelling in clay, whittling are all ways that have helped older people to deal with the frustrations and injustices of old age. Music or singing can often assuage anger. Keeping a diary is another way of expressing anger; it does no harm, and may do a lot of good. Being able to share anger in a proper way is also creative. Telling someone else about one's fury at being treated 'like a silly old fool' is a healthy way of sharing an unpleasant episode that has recently happened.

Physical exercise, if one is well enough to indulge in it, is another good way of dealing with anger. Unfortunately some older people cannot use this option, but slamming a door, or going out into the corridor for a short walk may offer relief.

Serious anger, amounting to verbal or physical violence, between older people and younger carers almost always merits outside help. That help sometimes has to be quite firm. Day care once or twice a week may give some relief to a tired relative. The older person may benefit from a different atmosphere and from meeting professional carers who are not emotionally involved in their situation and/or tangled relationships. Organizations such as Age Concern[13] and Crossroads[14] are sometimes able to provide 'sitters' so that caring relatives can go out of the home for short periods. Respite care *on a regular basis* may help loving, but exhausted, spouses and relatives to keep their elderly and dependent relatives at home. Permanent removal may seem a sad expedient, but it is sometimes one that is justified.

Conclusion

The care of older people's spirits is not easy. It is not easy for the older person who still feels mentally young. It is not easy for any individual who is only too aware that important faculties are being lost. It is not at all easy for relatives and friends to watch someone who is deteriorating in health. Very old age is no fun. It is one of the most challenging times of a person's life. All-round understanding and sensitivity are needed if older people are to live happy and fulfilled lives in later life.

How can people know that they are having a happy and fulfilled life in later life? A healthy human spirit in an older person declares itself in circumventing the accepted hazards of older age. It will not worry unduly about that which cannot be changed. It will use humour to keep a healthy sense of proportion about life. It will use beauty to foster a sense of wonder. It will be eager to preserve as many good relationships as possible. People will form these relationships, even if the only living creatures they have seen today are a dried-up plant, or an ant scurrying across the kitchen. They will know how to cope with anxiety, guilt, depression and anger. They will find some peace of mind, even in distressing circumstances. They will cultivate a sense of wonder. Wonder expands people's horizons and sometimes takes them into reverent awe. Those who care for elderly people will find much satisfaction in enabling them to live to their fullest possible potential. They will show their love and respect by helping older people to retain as much independence and dignity as possible. They will be aware of an older person's need for wonder and peace of mind right to the end of their conscious lives.

6

Making Choices in Later Life

Our name will be forgotten in time,
and no one will remember our works;
our life will pass away like the traces of a cloud,
and be scattered like mist
that is chased by the rays of the sun
and overcome by its heat.
For our allotted time is the passing of a shadow
and there is no return from our death,
because it is sealed up and no one turns back.

(Wisdom 2.4–5)[1]

I call heaven and earth to witness against you today that I have set before you life and death, blessings and curses. Choose life so that you and your descendants may live, loving the Lord your God, obeying him, and holding fast to him; for that means life to you and length of days.

(Deuteronomy 30.19–20a)[2]

The Role of Religious Faith and its Companion Doubt in Making Choices

The rather lengthy biblical quotations that head this chapter have a specific purpose that is not necessarily religious. They are put there to accentuate the difficulties of making choices in later life. They highlight the extent to which belief and disbelief, trust and distrust, faith and doubt, matter when it comes to making important choices.

The first passage from the Wisdom of Solomon is a collection of ancient written and oral sayings. They were written down in this form about a century before the birth of Christ. In the book the author speaks of wisdom. He sees wisdom not just as a human attribute, but also as a gift that comes from outside, from God, Creator. In those times most people took the existence of God for granted, but some did not. The words in the quotation are ones that the writer put into the mouths of the unbelievers of his time. Those who took the views expressed in this quotation are saying that there is only one life to be lived. Just before the quoted passage, the unbelievers say that when they are dead, 'the spirit will dissolve like empty air'.[3] Obviously, if there is no God, no life other than the material body, no real 'spirit', then choices will be made on a different basis from the choices that believers in God will make.

The writer of this apocryphal book was a firm believer in the God of Abraham, Isaac and Jacob. He was not so interested in the opinions of unbelievers. He would have agreed that wisdom comes from God and that it offers guidance. He thought that human beings have one choice. They can accept the guidance, or reject it. The writer of the passage in Deuteronomy had no doubt at all that God is always present in people's lives. God offers them choices between life and death, blessings and curses. He writes with assurance; he tells his readers exactly how they can choose life through loving God above all things and obeying God.

People who are living in the twenty-first century often have great difficulty in hearing passages from the Bible like this. They reflect a time in human history when attitudes towards God, towards the Bible, towards laws like the Ten Commandments, offered a safe passage through life, and beyond life. God for believers has authority over their lives. Wisdom that comes from God is a gift that comes from God. It can be accepted or rejected. It all sounds so simple. Life in the twenty-first century does not seem like that to most people. There are scores of choices to be made in postmodern societies that did not need to be made at all at a time in human history when the world was underpopulated, not overpopulated. In the centuries immediately before and after the birth of Christ, people simply did not have the huge variety of choices that individuals are confronted with today. It affects everyone alive today because the choices that human beings make today are going to affect the quality of life of their grandchildren and great-grandchildren. Choices matter to everyone alive, for they affect the future of the planet in ways that did not exist before the Age of Enlightenment. The choices that people living in 'high-tech' industrialized countries do now matter.

So choice is an important matter for people at all stages of life. There are some influences that are important to all people who are making choices. One has already been mentioned: it matters whether or not a person believes in God when it comes to making choices. The balance between religious faith and doubt will affect people's way of making choices.

This is particularly so for older people. They have to make important choices about how they are going to live after retirement from work. They have to decide where they are going to live. They have to ask the most difficult question of all: when are they going to move away from independence to some form of dependency? Then there are still more questions that are less easily voiced. Many older people now have to make choices about how they want to die. Finding a balance between personal beliefs and doubts will affect even more people in the future, if everyone is given the right to decide when they want to die.

The influence of religious beliefs on people's choices is put first in this chapter because the present older generation had an upbringing in a time when the substructure of British society was still predominately Christian. Therefore, most people over eighty years old today will still make choices that are to some extent faith based, even if their faith is heavily compromised by doubt.

Human beings have a tendency to swing between faith and doubt. This proposition was put in quite a humorous way by the poet Robert Browning. in his poem, 'Bishop Blougram's Apology'. By the time Browning came to write this poem in the nineteenth century, religion was already less influential in people's lives than it had been in biblical times. In this long poem Bishop Blougram talks to a non-believer. He enters deeply into the mind of Gigadibs, the unbeliever, and identifies with him:

> And now what are we? Unbelievers both,
> Calm and complete, determinately fixed
> Today, tomorrow and for ever, pray?
> You'll guarantee me that? Not so, I think!
> In no wise! all we've gained is, that belief,
> As unbelief before, shakes us by fits,
> Confounds us like its predecessor.[4]

Browning goes on to illustrate ways in which both belief and disbelief can be shattered by experience. Since the bishop is determined to put forward the advantages of belief he adds:

> All we have gained then by our unbelief
> Is a life of doubt diversified by faith,
> For one of faith diversified by doubt:
> We called the chess-board white – we call it black.[5]

Faith and doubt are inseparable. Each needs the other. If either are quenched it will not be possible to play with excitement on the chessboard of life. Human beings grow by testing faith against doubt. Wise people know that both are vital to the well-being of the human spirit. Indeed, some people, like the Japanese writer and poet, Miguel de Unamuno y Jugo (1864–1936), go further. He says, 'Life is doubt, and faith without doubt is death.'[6]

Unamuno is speaking about faith and doubt as universals, rather than as qualities that are specifically religious. He draws his readers' attention to the difficulties of defining words in today's world as they were defined when they were first used.

For faith does not necessarily mean religious faith. Faith in the universal sense is closer to trust and trust is a quality that people need in life. Faith and trust are both in short supply in the twenty-first century. There is widespread distrust of authority figures such as politicians, faith leaders, government members, medical doctors and other figures who have power over ordinary people's lives. Trust in oneself, in others, in institutions is a matter of choice and balance. A measure of distrust is essential to making choices that are either beneficial or harmful.

The Role of Trust and Distrust in Making Choices

The difference between faith, in its religious sense, and the universal quality of trust is made clear by a simple example, taken from an everyday situation in real life.

Consider a child of five years old who is about to cross a road for the first time by herself. She has been taught by her parents to look both ways. She must listen for oncoming traffic, then look both ways again, listen again and then cross. Her life is in her own hands. To cross that road she has to believe in her own judgement. She needs to trust herself to cross that road without falling down under oncoming traffic. Otherwise she will not cross that road. She will remain static. She will become completely dependent on other people's judgement. She may be wise enough to go to a traffic crossing with lights. She still has to trust that car drivers will heed the red light and stop. She has to put her belief to the test; but she also needs to have a modicum of distrust. If she has no doubts at all about her judgement, or capacity to cross the road alone, she may cross safely, but she may not.

The child is only on that pavement kerb because of the judgement of her parents and the degree of responsibility they exercise in allowing her to go out alone. Parents who never trust their children may overprotect children from the kerbstones of life. They may impede the maturing of their offspring. Parents may also allow their children too much freedom of choice before they are ready for it. They may one day receive the awful news that their child has been run over, is seriously injured or has been killed. Hesitation or overconfidence may result in disaster. Human beings are constantly having to find the balance between trust and distrust when they make choices.

The child is not alone on that pavement. She is there because her parents either trust that she is capable of judgement, or because they simply do not care enough to know where she is. Moreover, her life does not depend solely on her, or on her parents. It also depends upon other people, car drivers, pedestrians, those who might snatch her out of danger should she fall. It depends upon local communities providing safe crossings, upon local legislators who determine speed limits, upon the priorities that governments place upon road safety.

Trust and Distrust as Dynamic Qualities in Human Development and in People's Ability to Make Choices

The story of the child crossing a road is a simple illustration of how human trust works. It works through individuals, through other people, through the sensible laws that govern society. Trust is dynamic; it grows, it changes as people become more mature. It interacts with consciousness, memory and experience. People's self-confidence, their ability to trust themselves, can also be severely impaired by past events, fears, illness or other people's reaction to them. Distrust and lack of self-confidence are disabling.

At the beginning of life, when children are physically and emotionally dependent on adults, those children tend to trust adults wholeheartedly. Later on young people learn the virtue of distrust in certain circumstances. Disappointments in adults, doubts about their veracity or reliability, encourage them to take more responsibility for themselves. As they grow into adult life they face the great questions about the reason for human existence, its purpose and ultimate goal.

Some young people who have spent their early years in adverse environments grow up full of suspicion and distrust.

Consequently they may become antisocial in their behaviour. They constantly challenge authority. They believe that they are unloved and unworthy of love. Great suffering in childhood can predispose children to grow into rebellious adults. They may want to inflict the suffering they have endured on those who caused it.

It is known, for instance, that a fairly high proportion of people who have been sexually abused in childhood become adult abusers. If, however, they meet other people who not only love them but trust in them, their lives may be transformed by the encounter. Such encounters can also predispose young people to commit their lives to the relief of suffering. A sizeable number of abused children will grow up to become medical doctors, nurses and social workers. Early conditioning and experience does affect the way in which people become who they are when they grow into adult life. That does not necessarily mean that human beings are programmed. Most people think that they can make choices. They can choose to trust themselves and other people, or they can choose to live in cynical distrust of themselves, as well as of others.

By the time adolescents become young adults they have a considerable amount of experience of life to build upon. They may choose to trust in themselves and in others with whom they interact. They, and older adults, are often faced by doubts as to whether what they are being told is fact. They question the truth of statements that come from someone whom they do not know well enough to trust. If they are fortunate enough to live in an industrialized society of the northern hemisphere, their education will help them to develop confidence in their own judgement. They will learn to meet other people's judgements by making choices between distrust and trust of the person speaking, based on their previous experiences of the person in question.

Experience improves the balance between trust and distrust. If someone makes a promise and does not keep it, the fruit of that promise will taste bitter. Disappointment may deter a person from further trust. On the other hand, one bitter apple does not mean that the next one will be equally bitter; consequently, one person may decide to trust the other person again. There is another choice: one person may not trust another, but may still decide to continue the relationship.

Once people have gained some maturity, they make choices every day without thinking very much about them. They have found their balance between unquestioning trust and complete scepticism. Since it has become habitual for them to make choices in a fairly fixed pattern, other people may judge them to be either naïve, or cynical. Yet, at any time the balance may change. When it does, it may have profound effects on people's lives. An 'own familiar friend',[7] one they have loved, and in whom they have in the past placed much trust, may turn against them, betray them or destroy their happiness. They may then become unable to trust in anyone again, either for a long time, or for ever.

Elderly people have been moulded by all kinds of external influences and by their inner responses to those influences. By the time they reach retirement age they will generally have attained a consistent pattern of behaviour that expresses their personality. They may have settled into habits and ways of life that are congenial to them, if not to others. Younger people tend to think that older people are who they are because of who they have been. Older people are often thought to be incapable of change, or very unlikely to change. That is not a universal law of nature. Elderly people can change, and do change, because the human spirit is never static. So long as people live there is always a dynamic at work between faith and doubt that may change the balance between the two at any moment.

Genes, 'Original Sin', 'Original Goodness' and Moral Choices

John O'Donohue's working definition of the human spirit in Chapter 2 is worth repetition. He said that the human spirit is the 'ultimate and intimate signature' of people's individuality. It is 'the source from which consciousness, experience and memory unfold, and to which they return'.[8] Genes partly determine people's individuality. They modify choices. Environments, specially those of the womb and of young children's formative years, affect later decisions. Individuals have some control over who they want to become. The interaction of trust and distrust, faith and doubt, nourishes the human spirit. These dynamic elements influence human beings' moral stances in life.

It has been said that human beings are moral animals:

> The notion of person-hood identifies a category of morally considerable beings that is thought to be coextensive with humanity.[9]

Immanuel Kant thought of personhood 'as the quality that makes a being valuable and thus morally considerable'.[10] Developmental philosophers and psychologists have been increasingly interested in this aspect of human behaviour. They are interested in a human being's attitudes towards the rest of creation, animate and inanimate. They ask challenging questions to the Christian Churches in particular. People of religious faith need to develop a satisfactory theological anthropology if they are to give well-considered answers to the questions that many people are now asking. Those questions concern the nature and scope of human morality. They challenge the assumption that human beings are the only moral animals in the world, and that moral behaviour towards other human beings is the only moral behaviour that matters. Those who think in that way believe that they do not, therefore, need to act morally towards creation itself, or towards members of the animal and plant kingdoms. Creation, plants and animals are not 'moral being': they exist only for the use of people. Many philosophers and some people of profound religious faith, however, are now putting forward a contrary view. Some assert that, 'a morally considerable being is a being who can be wronged in the morally relevant sense'.[11] That widens the responsibility of human beings towards creation, animals and plants. Others contradict all that has been said. They state that human beings are animals, amoral beings. All morality is defined and taught by human beings. The arguments are likely to continue for a long time.

One way to approach these difficult questions is to look at the role of choice in moral behaviour. Human genes predispose people to find balance between polarities, between life and death, between self and 'outside self', between stasis and action. Creation itself is a process of growth and multiplication, death and decay. Relatedness is a feature of existence. Stillness and activity are part of the dynamics of living creatures. Polarity is a precious gift of creation as the tension between opposites holds them in balance.

Human babies are born with genes that predispose them to particular patterns of behaviour, but they are also born with a potential for choice. Some may not have the genetic identity, or the capacity to mature sufficiently, to be able to make effective choices, but the potential is there. There are a relatively few people who dissent from the idea that human beings have some capacity to make choices. They assert that human beings are nothing more than live programmed robots.

Human Responsibility for Making Choices

The need to make choices is stressful, so human beings have often sought advice from outside themselves. They do this to make choices that will benefit them, or something, or someone, about whom they care. That 'other' whose help is sought may be another human being, words in a book, a figure from the past or that ultimate entity whom people name as God. It is perfectly possible to be a moral person without believing in God, although religious belief can sometimes assist moral choices.

Human beings sometimes think and act in contradictory ways. If human beings have free will they can make informed choices. That means that the human spirit is not amoral by nature. It is, nevertheless, apparent that human beings can choose to live in amoral ways. They can and do hold that there is no such thing as a 'good choice' or an 'evil choice'. They may, or may not, believe that 'original goodness', or 'original sin', are a part of human genetic inheritance. People who disown ideas of 'original sin' are often able to accept that human beings are born into the moral climate of the prevalent culture. Individuals may dissent from their inherited moral culture. They often do so by contesting the choices that seem to be dominant in their own particular environment. Through action they shift the balance of their choices in one direction or the other. Choices between different forms of power, for instance, lead to anarchy, hierarchy and democracy. These are all ways of life that human beings adopt as they struggle to find the freedom to live their choices.

Atheists who decide to live without any idea of an outside identity called God can make moral choices. Twentieth-century Absurdists, for instance, held to the philosophical proposition that life is cruel, ludicrous and ultimately futile. That view influenced the way they made choices. Atheists who categorically state that there is no God, no Creator, no Source of morality, can still believe in a collective way of life that is beneficial to humankind. They will aim to contribute to that way of life through their actions. Humanists will strive for the betterment of humankind. That principle informs their moral choices.

Many people alive today say that they simply do not know if there is a God. They may decide to act as if there was God, or as if there were not. Their decision will affect their behaviour. In the present culture of Britain there are two prevalent fashions that diminish humanity. One is embodied in the words, 'I can't help it', as if people had no personal responsibility for their actions. The other is, 'It's their fault.' People are often quick to accuse others of being irresponsible. These ideas come from a widespread abrogation of absolutist morality. This is coupled with a failure to establish a collective morality that can provide agreed guidelines for individual and collective responsibility for the world.

Environmental Influences that Affect Human Choices

The immediate family and community culture that human beings are born into are the starting points for the environmental influences that influence an individual's life. They are, however, not the settled, or end points, of people's moral choices. It is apparent from a study of early world history that human beings have long sought to find meaning and purpose in life. Many, though not all, reach out to put their trust in something that seems to be greater than themselves or their immediate community. They consciously choose a balance between faith and doubt. That balance is loaded towards trust; trust in a collective belief. They adopt a way of life that embodies a personal way of life that amounts to faith. Among some people religious faith also contributes negatively or positively to the choices they make.

The Role of Religious Faith in Older People's Lives

In this chapter 'faith' is not necessarily synonymous with religious belief. Yet religious faith does enhance many people's abilities to live their lives to the full. These people rely on their religious beliefs to help them to make everyday choices. Religious faith can be an important factor in many people's lives. It helps them to become the people they would like to be. It can act positively to reinforce faith and trust in oneself, and in other people. It can act negatively when it leads to suspicion, undue condemnation and distrust of oneself, and of other people.

When people reach the later years of their lives they will still have the same genes as those with which they were born. However, they will have interacted with and related to creation and creatures outside themselves all their lives. Their genes will be the same, but they will have become what they now are partly through their experiences of relatedness in time, space and eternity. William Wordsworth, the eighteenth-century poet, put it elegantly:

My heart leaps up when I behold
   A rainbow in the sky:
So was it when my life began;
So is it now I am a man;
So be it when I shall grow old,
   Or let me die!
The Child is father of the Man;
And I could wish my days to be
Bound each to each by natural piety.[12]

That is a challenging thought. A colleague recently commented that he would be a very different person if he had not learnt to trust in himself and in others. He said that, left to himself, he would be a disgruntled old person. He would be moaning over past failures, thwarted ambitions, enmities, irreducible suffering. Had he retained his youthful opinions, he would now be intolerantly critical of people and cultures that were not to his liking. Certainly he would be hostile to people of other religious faiths. He was, he said, thankful that adversity in his younger years had prompted him to formulate a faith. He had tried to live by that faith. His religious faith had reinforced his fundamental faith in his chosen way.

In Britain religious faith is still strong in some localities and regions. At the same time it seems to be in overall decline in its influence on society. The growth of fundamentalism in every religion has weakened many people's adherence to, and admiration for, religious institutions that deny freedom of expression and choice. Some people do feel safe if they live strictly enclosed by absolutist doctrines. Many young people start out their lives in that kind of way. People of religious faith sometimes change. As they mature they may see the effects of strict adherence to absolutist doctrines. Their views become more inclusive, more tolerant, more compassionate. Others, however, use religious ideas to reinforce prejudice. They can become intolerant, even antagonistic, towards people who do not share their 'hardline views'.

These changes in people's attitudes towards organized institutional religions have had profound effects on the moral climate of affluent societies. Many people, including some of strong religious faith, find themselves more in tune with their own home-made faith. They no longer want to live by the tenets of mainline religious institutions. Familiar words and rituals of worship have long since gone from their memories, or been overlaid by new forms of worship services. Unless clerics and ministers of religion are sensitive to older people's needs, their spirits are left unnourished. Alone, they will face one of the greatest challenges that will have happened to them since their birth: they have to come to terms with loss of independence, dying and death.

The Role of Trust and Distrust, Faith and Doubt in Making Important Choices in Later Life

So far, most of this chapter has been an introduction to two difficult questions. How does trust in oneself, in human nature, in communities and in society operate in the lives of older people? How can distrust work positively? How can religious faith help older people to make difficult choices?

Older people are familiar with other people's distrust about their capacity to make choices. They are thought to need protection. They are sometimes treated as children who have not yet developed to the point of being able to make choices for themselves. They may become isolated in ways that make it difficult for them to join in activities outside their homes. They are ignored. So they take matters into their own hands.

Many older people rebel against becoming passive and dependent on other people. They protest vigorously when they are denied access to certain treatments because of their age.[13] They march when they consider that their pension provisions are unjust. They lobby Parliament in ways that were quite rare in former times. Then, pensioners trusted Parliament and local governments' welfare organizations to deal justly with them. Now they do not. Distrust has spurred them into action. It has worked positively for it has helped older people to trust in themselves. Older people now have more choice about how they want to live and what they want to do, certainly in the early years of retirement.

Active protest by older people in Britain, during the last twenty years or so, has had effect. Voluntary organizations are caring for the welfare of senior citizens in ways that nourish the human spirit. They have brought pressure to bear on local councils and governments to notice the needs of disadvantaged people. Greatly improved accessibility has been a key to a more pleasurable life for many elderly and disabled people. Provisions under the Disablement Act[14] have enabled more of them to participate in ventures that were formerly denied to them. It has needed legislation to bring this about, but it has happened within the last half-century. It helps to provide for the spiritual needs of many older people. In Britain, cheap fares for people over the age of sixty have made it possible for older people to travel without bringing themselves to penury. Disabled people can now socialize and integrate into their local community. They can visit churches, libraries, cinemas, lunch clubs and meetings with the help of 'door-to-door' bus services, commonly known as 'Ring and ride'. Public opinion has mobilized support. Individuals and organizations like Age Concern,[15] Help the Aged[16] and other agencies have persuaded local councils and governments to begin to meet the needs of disadvantaged people in society.

Many people who are now approaching later life grew up in a society where authority figures and caring institutions were thought to be worthy of trust. Society is no longer the same as the one they once knew. They now find themselves living in a very different society, one in which distrust is rife, and where they are having to make difficult choices. Yet they no longer feel able to trust those who declare themselves to be 'experts in care' and trustworthy, but who are often found to be untrustworthy and fallible.

Some of the biggest choices older people have to make are about when to give up driving and when to move away from independence to some degree of dependency. An older man is told by his son to give up driving. He protests. How can he do that? He needs the car to take his wife shopping. Should he trust his son's motives? Perhaps his son wants to take over the car? One child may offer a home to an elderly widow. The other children are united in declaring that she should retain her own home and independence with the help of the social services. She turns to her doctor for advice. He says she should consider sheltered accommodation. How can she trust that advice when she hardly knows him, certainly not as she knew her old doctor? The old lady feels confused and uncertain. She has a little dog, whom she takes out for short walks every day. Many places of sheltered accommodation do not accept pets. So she clings to her home obstinately. She finds herself infected with distrust.

These are typical choices that face many older people, and they are difficult to make. Often the choices are so bewildering, and so difficult to make, that they are postponed indefinitely. Instead older people look for creative ways of remaining independent and productive.

Maintaining Independence and Building up Self-esteem

There is more to caring for the human spirit, one's own or other people's, than protest. It goes deeper than securing changes that benefit older people. Individuals who are aware of increasing years often find great resources within themselves. Older, even very elderly, people may continue to be creative in many different ways. A ninety-seven-year-old friend has only just stopped creating beautiful cross-stitch embroidery because she cannot now see clearly enough to produce work that satisfies her. Many quite elderly people produce beautiful tapestries, paintings, sculptures, photographs that take people's breath away when they are exhibited in public. Betty, an eighty-six-year-old retired missionary,[17] joined an art class in her late seventies and is still enjoying it. She organizes a lively discussion group in a neighbour's home. She is also inventive in her way of stimulating creativity in one of her oldest friends who suffers from increasing loss of memory. Peter, an older friend of some years standing,[18] insists on writing letters to clergy and bishops. He is distressed because his church takes little notice of some older members of the congregation. They would prefer to worship in the old ways. They have to learn new ways of worship whether they want to or not. Having to pay so much attention to words on a printed page prevents them from allowing familiar words and rituals to carry them into silent adoration. He may be a nuisance to the hierarchy, but it is a creative way of using his anger. He has Church law on his side: it is still legal to use the Book of Common Prayer in the Anglican Church to which he belongs. Given a bit of good will, it should still be able to satisfy the needs of elderly people at least once a week, if not on a Sunday.

It is apparent from listening to older people in different parts of the country that they need to prepare for their later years long before they reach them. Individuals can adopt self-help schemes to help them stay physically and socially active before they stop paid employment. In the two or three years before retirement many people benefit from retirement courses, information about pension rights, health care, welfare, economic and social issues that affect people in their later years. Individuals can also nurture the human spirit fruitfully if they develop creative spiritual activities when they are growing older, but are not yet old. There is no absolute rule about this. It is never too late to attend to one's deepest needs. It *is* possible to live to the full even in adversity. A time will come, however, when the choice cannot be postponed any longer.

This is one of the most demanding choices any older person ever has to make. They need to be patient with themselves as they hover between staying in their own home and moving to a 'granny flat' in one of their children's or friend's homes, sheltered accommodation or a residential home. They also need other people to be patient with them as they try to come to the right decision. Unfortunately, it is not always possible to give older people the time they need.

Decisions are often precipitated by a stay in a geriatric ward of a local hospital. Relatives and hospital staff alike may feel that the older person needs residential care. The infirm patient resists. The hospital needs the bed for another patient. Pressure is brought on patient and/or relatives to 'find a more suitable long-term place'. Eventually the old person gives in, often against his or her better judgement. Sometimes it is wisely suggested that the older person go for a temporary stay somewhere to see if they like it enough to stay. This sometimes results in a happy outcome for patients and relatives alike. The human spirit can and does often adapt to changed circumstances.

The Role of Caring Agencies in Assisting People to Make Choices in Later Life that can Nourish the Human Spirit

Once the difficult choice has been made to move from independent living in one's own home to some form of dependency, there are still more choices to be made. Some elderly people are so upset by the thought of residential care that they choose to try sheltered accommodation when they are not independent enough to live in that kind of a place. Living in sheltered accommodation is an excellent choice for those who know they are getting too old to live alone, but are still active. That means being able to do their own shopping, cook for themselves and take care of themselves with some minimal help from relatives, home helps and local social services. They know that going into such sheltered housing will prolong the time when they can look after themselves properly. Sheltered housing is not so good for people who cannot manage to take care of their personal needs. Making the wrong choice can lead to much misunderstanding and unhappiness for everyone concerned.

When the choice eventually has to be made to move to a residential home or a nursing home, it is still important to allow as much choice as possible. Individuals can achieve a great deal as long as they remain independent. Elderly residents in sheltered accommodation, however, are not always able to go out of doors. Those in residential homes, nursing homes and hospitals are not usually independent. They need their spiritual nourishment brought to them. It is not enough to be kind to older people who are housebound.

A survey of residential homes shows that attention to the human spirits of the people who live in them is patchy. In some homes it is very good indeed. There are opportunities for shared activities such as gentle 'keep-fit classes'. There are opportunities for communal games such as scrabble, whist and bridge, all of which stimulate the mind. Books are provided. Excursions are arranged, some of which might satisfy people's spiritual needs. There are opportunities for sitting in the sunshine in the garden. There are people and organizations that visit. There are opportunities for worship. All these are wonderfully capable of nourishing residents' spirits.

On the other hand, there are places where elderly residents are brought into a communal room, whether they like it or not. They have to sit within sight and sound of a television set until lunchtime. Afterwards, those who are fortunate may escape back to their bedrooms for an afternoon nap. Small wonder that some people in such situations decide to withdraw. They remain in their rooms for as much of the day as possible. There they can at least listen to the music of silence.

Most of what has been said in the preceding paragraphs has come from the experience of visiting elderly people in residential situations. It has sometimes been possible to listen, and to grow angry enough to try to change things. Throughout a long working life there has been great sympathy for hard-worked staff who simply have too little time to care for the spiritual and faith needs of those in their care. Nevertheless a great deal can still be done to arrange a good quality of life and spiritual care.

The Role of Voluntary and Statutory Agencies in Caring for the Human Spirit in Later Years

It is evident from talking to individuals and to representatives of caring agencies that the spiritual care of older people should start in middle age, not in old age. All the voluntary agencies mentioned so far focus on the care of the human spirit. They provide good faith care as well.

A good illustration of the beneficial changes that began to happen in the latter part of the twentieth century comes from a volunteer. In early retirement she became a 'buddy'. A 'buddy' is a volunteer from outside the immediate family and caring agencies. Her task was to befriend a man suffering from Alzheimer's disease. On undertaking this work she was required to attend a series of training sessions. She went to the local community psychiatric hospital for several months. Those with knowledge and long experience taught her invaluable lessons and skills. They not only helped her care for her friend. They prolonged her own active life, and helped her to maintain a lively interest in the problems of society.

A look at some of the charities working in this field, such as Age Concern, shows how much is being done to train volunteers who care for elderly people. There are many agencies who run good schemes. The following merit attention: the Methodist Homes' Centre for the Spirituality of the Ageing,[19] the Anglican Church Army[20] and a project called *Psalm*,[21] that operates in the Edmonton area of Greater London. These are all agencies that show great imagination in their approach to work with elderly people. All have training schemes for those younger retired older people who care for the elderly.

These agencies, and many more, have schemes for involving older people as volunteers. They have realized that older people are a valuable resource in any community. *Psalm*, for instance, has given training to older church members in pastoral visiting. Trained volunteers now undertake pre- and post-baptismal visiting. They lead discussion groups. They keep churches open during the daytime. They visit bereaved people. *Psalm*, and many other agencies working in more secular fields, have realized that properly selected and well-trained older volunteers can minister effectively in many areas of social life.

Good voluntary agencies stress the importance of inter-generational contact. The company and stimulation provided by younger people is beneficial to the spirits of older people.

Younger people also benefit from their contact with elderly persons. The Cambridge University Student Community Action, for instance, has seventy or more volunteering opportunities for students. One of them is called *Contact*.[22] It brings university students into contact with older Cambridge residents. One of the organizers, Jonathan Conlin, has commented in print: 'Many of our students start with a desire to indulge a social conscience, but they soon find that there are real benefits in having contact with someone outside the university cocoon.'[23]

Conclusion

Individuals and all faith agencies, both secular and religious, are aware of the importance of social inclusion as a way of ameliorating the loneliness, frustration and depression that are common among old people who are housebound or in residential care. They try to help older people to find meaning in life, to give them time for the discussion of problems, to help them maintain links with changing patterns in society. They encourage creativity among the elderly. Encouraging creativity is one of the most important ways of helping the spirit to flourish in older age and in later life.

When efforts to demonstrate compassion and justice towards old people become visible, the marks of a truly civilized society are beginning to be present. Today, Western societies are making those efforts but there is still much to be achieved.

7

Some Ethical Issues of Later Life

Ageism is rife.[1]

Every view of the world which does not include death or deliberately ignores it can only be an illusion.[2]

(Olivier Clément)

There were two posters on the walls of a waiting room. They were in a district hospital in Britain. One of these was of a mature woman with grey hair and kind eyes. Underneath her portrait there was a caption. The substance of its words was: 'I am not your "dear". "I am not your "luv". I am not who you think I am. I am usually known as Dr Elliot.' The other poster depicted Nelson Mandela and Winston Churchill. The caption said: 'Over the hill?' The phrase, 'ageism is rife', quoted at the beginning of this chapter, accompanied each of these posters. The implication was that however old people look, however old they are, they are human beings who are of value and should be treated as such.

Institutional Ageism

It is good to know that the Department of Health is doing what it can to counter the current attitudes in British society towards older people. The posters draw attention to some of the iniquities of ageism. There is an increasing awareness among the general population about the destructive nature of materialism, consumerism, racism, sexism and classism. All these 'isms' focus on differences between two or more sets of people. They imply that one set of people is considered to be more deserving, important, or more valuable than another. 'Isms' of various kinds are widely used in our society to promote the interests of one set of people by denigrating another definable group of people.

Ageism is an attitude of mind, reinforced by structural discrimination. It affects people of every age. Young people can find themselves universally distrusted simply because some of their number are disruptive in social situations. The antisocial behaviour of a relatively few young people becomes stereotyped. Hostility towards a few offenders becomes transferred on to all young people in an unfair way.

'We do not employ women of childbearing age,' a middle-aged woman said recently during a British election campaign.[3] She saw nothing wrong in what she was saying. It made common sense to her. Her business could not afford the long gap of maternity leave and the payment of benefits. Yet, by excluding a group of people because of their age the employer was ignoring an important fact. A gifted person of childbearing age might not be able to have children, but might well be an ideal employee. Young women looking for employment might well feel offended by their arbitrary exclusion because, it is sometimes hinted, 'all young women are likely to breed like rabbits'.

Ageism affects older working people and people who are living on pensions more than younger people. It is common to hear statements like this: 'We do not employ people over fifty.' Sensitive employers may avoid the issue of age: 'I'm sorry, but you have had work, you know; there are so many younger people who have never worked.' Sometimes an employer will say to an older person: 'We need you to move on, so that a stronger person can replace you.' It is well known that people over fifty years old find it difficult to get long-term employment. The consequence is that those older people who still need to earn money dye their hair and tidy up their wrinkles.

They pretend they have inexhaustible energy. They lie about their age on their application forms, or at interview.

Once citizens become old enough to take their pensions, they are often treated as if they were redundant in society. These attitudes occur in families, communities and society. Many people who are on pensions defy the cultural norms. They involve themselves in a wide variety of voluntary activities, but too often they are treated as if they were of little value. Their occupational skills and their great experience of life are not properly used, nor is their advice heeded. That *is* a generalization, but it is remarkable how many older people feel sidelined by society.

In a century where more and more people are living to great ages, it is apparent that scientific discoveries and advances in knowledge have tipped the balance of nature. That may be a very good thing for individual members of society. It means, however, that many people are going to draw pensions, or need financial help of other kinds, for longer than they used to a century or two ago. Consequently, industrial societies with high rates of longevity find themselves in a muddle; not only in a muddle, but also in a crisis.

Society and Longevity

Governments, finding themselves with an increasingly ageing population, may respond to the problems by moving the goalposts. One response is to delay the pensionable age by law. More people then go on working and paying taxes for longer. Governments may latch on to this idea since it makes some economic sense. Retirement ages are raised, although it is well known that ageing takes place at variable rates in individuals, although some kinds of work exact more toll on strength than others.

Dictatorial statements about retirement ages are unlikely to be popular. It should be possible to have a flexible retiring age over a ten-year span. This would take care of factors like physical strength, the stress levels of different employments and individual circumstances. Inflexible retirement ages are unworkable. It should not be necessary to 'go sick' to secure 'early' retirement.

Raising retirement ages may seem attractive to governments, but this measure will not be sufficient to cope with the problems of longevity. So governments may also apply other stringent measures to deal with the current situation. In one affluent industrialized society the government is trying to assign the responsibility for saving money for the later years of life to individuals. It does not want to continue the former policy of aiming for joint responsibility between employees, employers and the state. Employees are sometimes encouraged to opt out of company pension schemes, where both employees and employers contribute into pension funds. Short-term gain in the pay packet is a convenient way of blurring the long-term consequences of such actions. Instead, employees are urged to make private pension arrangements. Occasionally, huge companies, with scant concern for the welfare of their employees, manage to divert pension funds to less long-term projects. They virtually steal their employees' money. Government denies any responsibility for these disasters.

Over the past fifty years, people of all shades of political opinion have underestimated the effect of modern science on longevity. The consequences of this policy are now apparent among people who are older and no longer able to work. Hospital beds are blocked by older people. There are not enough residential homes or nursing homes for those who cannot pay for their care at the current high levels. In many English and Welsh counties individuals pay for personal care, whatever their circumstances. Those who cannot pay must do without care. A large number of old people are existing in relative poverty. Their poverty is relative, because no one is poor in the northern hemisphere compared to those who live in the southern hemisphere. More will join these relatively poor people in future generations. A better alternative is to rationalize the care systems of such countries so that the elderly poor have proper care. That may mean that affluent members of society have to contribute more to the care of elderly and disabled people.

The Role of Legislation in Older People's Lives

A society is judged by the way it cares for the poor, the physically and mentally disabled members of society and its old people. Industrialized societies, where the emphasis is laid on personal affluence, rising prosperity and higher standards of living, do not come out well when such criteria are applied to them. Yet, it would be wrong to deny governments their due credit, for life *is* better for pensioners than it was a hundred years ago

Legislation is one instrument of society that can be used to protect its most vulnerable members. Legislative efforts have been made, and are being made, by successive British governments to achieve more economic justice for older people. The focus is on those from the least affluent sections of society; the method used is to 'top up' benefits. All political parties now seem to want all older people to continue to benefit from reductions in fares, heating allowances and free television licences. Some proposals are also being made to reduce the burden of their council tax. These measures do improve the physical and economic welfare of older people. They do not directly attend to the needs of the human spirit: the need, for instance, to walk safely on the streets. Older people need to be treated with the dignity due to any human being. They need to be valued and wanted in the communities in which they live. Some of these spiritual needs can be protected in part by legislation. Legislation is, however, only one small part of what still needs to be achieved in a postmodern society.

Human nature is such that some individuals will always seek to exploit protective legislation. Those who exploit the system harm both the younger groups of older pensioners, and those who are of more advanced ages. Any tendency to excessive individualism is enhanced in a pluralist society where some people pay scant regard to the common good. Individualism is also prevalent in societies that are infected with a culture of blame.

Human beings alive today are skilled at talking about the present ills in their societies. Many of them talk vociferously about all that is wrong. Quite often they talk about what 'they' – anyone other than themselves – should do. In practice, the majority of people who see what is wrong are unable to do much to put a more positive view forward. Some individuals feel incompetent to 'take on' companies, corporations and governments. Others are unwilling, or unable, to do so. There are, it is true, a number of individuals who are willing to take on the political responsibilities that decide the legal infrastructures of society. Certainly, there are more people who do try to educate the whole population about the valuable contributions that older people can make to society. Where questions about the proper treatment of older people in society arise, it becomes apparent that there *is* a fine balance between individual responsibility and collective responsibility.

Many people, particularly from the more affluent sections of society, say that the pendulum has swung too far. They say that they do not want a 'nanny' state. People who hold this opinion say that individuals should take more responsibility for their lives and welfare. Unfortunately, it seems plain that the human race has not yet matured sufficiently to act voluntarily for the collective good of the weakest and most fragile of its citizens. Legislation *is* needed, but legislation cannot work miracles. The culture of a society or nation will largely determine the outcome of well-intentioned law-making.

Collective Responsibility for Social Attitudes Towards Older People

It matters not which government is in power. The problems remain because the majority of citizens alive in today's industrialized societies are no longer used to making sacrifices for the common good. They do not feel it necessary to be loyal either to their nation, or to the world, or to Planet Earth.

Governments make appeals to people's worst instincts rather than to their best, so that they can stay in power. It is not surprising that electorates become cynical and quite grasping in their own interests. Older and vulnerable people in society continue to suffer.

Despondency about human nature need not lead to passivity. The future is in the hands of all. There are signs that people are beginning to see that. Many want to do something to bring justice to older people. Tax cuts do not appeal so much when it means that older relatives and poorer people will be unable to receive the help they so urgently and patently need. It is still frequently possible to overhear men and women grumbling about the conditions under which they live, but a remarkable number will try to do something about it, however small. This is true, especially among old people themselves. Many of them are leading the way for the rest of the population.

Older people, some of whom are well over eighty years of age, work in every kind of welfare and charitable organization. Many older people care deeply about others. They help out their children; they care for their grandchildren. They are a hidden economic force in all industrialized societies. Many people of every generation are taking matters into their own hands. They are making considerable sacrifices for the well-being of vulnerable people in society. Moreover, they do not stop at their own families; and many older people give generously from small incomes. They support relief efforts among the impoverished peoples of the world as well as those afflicted by natural disasters. So governments, voluntary agencies and institutions of influence, like the media, need to nurture those efforts. They, too, can uphold any small or large efforts for justice. They, too, can protect those who are no longer able to fend for themselves as they did when they were able to work and earn their living.

Democracies may thrive on opposition. Many citizens, however, think that certain issues in society, like education, law and order, and health and social care, are better managed in a different way. Thorough non-adversarial debate might take place before parliamentary decisions on these issues. Then it might be possible for a civilized nation to achieve a greater degree of consensus. Perhaps humankind is not yet ready for such radical solutions to its humanitarian problems? Certainly, in a pluralistic, postmodern, multifaith and post-Christian society it is apparently not yet possible to achieve a common mind that will satisfy all citizens of any country in the northern hemisphere. Adversarial democracy continues to dominate political systems. It can only work effectively when political parties are both responsible and evenly matched. Electoral reform may be overdue if society as a whole is to find more effective ways of dealing with its problems.[4]

Contributions of Older People to Spiritual Values in Society

Older people in society guard some of the moral values in society. Younger people would do well to heed their wisdom and usually exemplary behaviour. It would not be right to go back to the puritanical, punitive attitudes that some former generations had towards moral transgressors. There is, however, a need for members of society to recover a sense of communal responsibility, and the majority of older people recognize that. There may come a time when the motivation of postmodern generations will not solely rely on punishment as a deterrent. Instead, national and local governments may combine encouragement to responsible citizens and punishment with rehabilitation to those who transgress the law. This kind of policy is already at work among some large corporations and commercial companies.[5]

The majority of citizens want to enjoy their lives as morally responsible people. Human nature is not as bad as it is sometimes made out to be. Given the opportunity, many people want to act for the collective good. This can only happen if there is a consensus about the need for a moral culture in society. Pluriform, industrial societies meet with considerable obstacles to the recovery of an agreed morality.

The institutions that guard moral behaviour in society are the faith communities, the government and the Law. Many of the current faith communities are beset by fundamentalism. They fear the loss of their identities. They are also afraid of becoming irrelevant to society. Instead they are apparently preoccupied with infighting about inessentials. They are trapped by their hostility towards one another. They are no longer able to speak for people's nascent moral sense. Governments hesitate between appeals to citizens' acquisitiveness and to their better nature. The Law does its best for individual justice, but is subject to pressures on every side. National and international judges frequently attract hostility rather than praise for their efforts to help citizens to live responsibly. Even the United Nations cannot act coherently when major nation members opt out of multinational decisions designed to protect the whole world from the consequences of some human behaviour.[6]

It is time for a change of attitudes among the population of industrialized countries. Changes in attitudes from individualism to consideration for the common good are always slow. People of retirement age are leading the way in society. They stand at the growing margin of society. They may be old-fashioned and somewhat fierce in their criticisms of younger people, but they have the wisdom of long experience behind them. They still have a great deal to offer to a society that has seemingly lost its way. They may be near to death, but they have a legacy to leave. They also care greatly about what will happen to future generations. Younger people may ignore them, but society as a whole would do well to listen to them. Many old people grew up in times when they were poor, really poor. They do not want to return to those conditions, but they do see value in living a little less affluently. Then others worse off than themselves could have a better standard of life, both in their own societies and in the world outside.

Radical Solutions to Longevity and Overpopulation

Some radical solutions to the problems of longevity in industrialized countries are on the horizon. Human beings in affluent countries consume more of the world's resources than is just. They live long lives. It is difficult for such nations and societies to find ways of helping people who live in the southern hemisphere to reach a more equitable way of life. In those poorer countries there is not enough food to eat. The death rate for young people is rising. Governments and intergovernmental agencies are aware of the problems. They are being prompted to action by public pressure. Educating governments and keeping up the public pressure on them is important, and will continue to be so.

Radical solutions, however, are frequently unjust to individuals. They are also unpopular. In 1798, Robert Malthus (1766–1834)[7] wrote his *Essay on the Principle of Population*. Since then, some people and nations have decided on stringent measures to control the size of their populations.[8] Some societies curtail their birth rates by law. Some nations have been willing to consider active euthanasia, the deliberate killing of aged and/or handicapped people, as a solution to some of the problems of eugenics and incapacitating longevity. Some have embarked on genocide. Seemingly, many nations, including the so-called 'civilized nations of the world', have ignored what is happening in the rest of the world. They have tolerated poverty, famine, the ravages of war and AIDS in distant countries. The balance of population in the world is altering. In certain populations in the southern hemisphere the young and strong are dying fast. Among them, a relatively few adults are left to care for very young, sick and infirm older people. The standard of living is falling. Faith communities, governments and multinational agencies may choose to ignore what is happening. If they continue to pursue such policies they will be guilty of systematic, selective elimination of some populations, while others continue to prosper. Moreover, if they pursue policies which destroy the environment they will end planetary life.

Society and the Relief of Suffering

The majority of people alive today do not think along such lines. They simply do not believe that present action to improve the lives of some people on earth has disastrous consequences for others. They do not heed scientists' warnings about the destruction of the environment because they cannot foresee that present actions affect the future of Planet Earth. Affluent industrialized societies see themselves as 'civilized', intelligent and compassionate. They also see themselves as better at the relief of undeserved suffering than they were two centuries ago. Most people alive today would support the relief of physical and mental pain for themselves and others without hesitation.

From the beginning of time many human beings have sought to relieve undeserved pain and suffering. Since the middle of the nineteenth century they have had better ways of ameliorating suffering. This has been one reason for a shift in attitudes towards undeserved suffering. Another substantial reason for the change in attitude has been the discarding of certain premises that were formerly acceptable.

In the northern hemisphere, before the mid-nineteenth century, suffering was widely held to have a spiritual function. It was used as a punishment for deserved suffering. This was a method of deterring others from misdemeanours and crimes. Retributive punishment protected the rest of society from serious crime. Restorative punishment could lead to improved behaviour.

Among Christians, undeserved suffering brought people close to Christ. Suffering could result in spiritual growth. God was sometimes seen as the author of suffering. Many efforts were made to stop the introduction of anaesthetics in childbirth. Those who opposed anaesthetics sometimes did so on the grounds that God ordained women's suffering because of Eve's Sin.[9] Even if God was not directly responsible for suffering, God tolerated it. It brought victims of sickness closer to Christ, who gave them strength to endure, and, if necessary, to die well.

People's attitudes towards the spiritual benefit of pain have changed to a considerable extent. Most people are now happy to accept pain relief for themselves and for other people. Many people see no value at all in prolonged or unusual pain. So it has become possible for many people to accept the termination of human life on humanitarian grounds.

The Termination of Life as a Humane Measure to Relieve Suffering

There are various ways of terminating human life humanely. At the outset of this discussion it is important to distinguish between 'passive euthanasia' and 'active euthanasia'. 'Passive euthanasia' is a deliberate effort to relieve suffering by the use of drugs and techniques that incidentally *might* hasten death, but will not necessarily do so. 'Active euthanasia' is the planned termination of human life by deliberate action to ensure death.

Moral considerations about ending human life should be kept distinct from parliamentary propositions to legalize the termination of life by medical intervention. Some people are supportive of 'passive euthanasia', even of 'active euthanasia'. They are, nevertheless, opposed to legalization that might open the door to unscrupulous killing for gain.

Medical doctors make a firm distinction between actions that do not involve heroic intervention to keep someone alive at all costs, and the use of drugs and medical interventions that might result in incidental death. In the latter instance they know that sometimes their attempts to relieve pain and suffering might incidentally shorten life. They state that such efforts are different from the deliberate killing of people who have asked to be 'put out of their misery'. They are also aware that 'active euthanasia' is different from killing someone who cannot request death, but seems to be beyond hope of living a sustainable existence. Killing an unconscious patient could be murder unless that eventually comes within the provisions of legalized euthanasia. Currently the medical and nursing professions do not seem to be so opposed to active euthanasia as they used to be. In July 2005, the British Medical Association narrowly voted to drop its opposition to Lord Joffe's 'Assisted Dying for the Terminally Ill Bill' that he intends to reintroduce within the next few years.[10] Many individual doctors and nurses, however, are still opposed to it.

Withholding Active Intervention

The first of these important areas of perplexity is summed up by Arthur Hugh Clough's aphorism. He said, 'Thou shalt not kill; but needs't not strive officiously to keep alive'.[11] Many people now appreciate that the quality of a person's life is as important as its length. They shrink from the idea of being kept artificially live when the balance between life and death has shifted irrevocably towards death. In that case the suffering and indignity of remaining alive may be great.

Many people trust their relatives and doctors enough to discuss their feelings about what they want to happen when they become terminally ill. That is enough for some people. They trust their doctors to do what is in their best interests. Many older people are happier to trust their own family doctors than hospital staff whom they do not know. The publicity given by the media to modern technology, however, can be gruesome for those who are not trained in modern medicine. Some professional and lay people have tried to ensure that patients have a more formal say in what happens when life might become intolerable. They have introduced the idea of 'living wills'[12] as a remedy.

Living wills are also known as 'advanced directives'. People can draw up documents that state that they do not want to be kept alive by heroic interventions. They can also state 'what types of medical treatment the maker of the statement does or does not desire to receive in specific circumstances should he, or she, be incapable of giving or refusing consent'. Living wills 'must be signed whilst the maker is mentally competent'.[13] Those who complete and sign such a statement can expect that their wishes will be taken into account when those in charge of their treatment must make life or death decisions.

Unlike attested 'last wills' about what happens to one's

property after death, 'living wills' have, at present, no force in law. They *are* respected by the medical profession, but they are not at present the sole determinant about whether, or not, to withhold life-saving treatment. Relatives who are told about 'living wills' before they are needed may find that knowledge helpful. Some older people feel that they do not want to live unless they can have a reasonable quality of life. What that constitutes varies from person to person. It is difficult to define. It must also be remembered that some relatives so dislike looking after their infirm and ageing relatives that they may bring pressure on them to make a 'living will'.

Professionals in the medical and nursing professions often find some difficulties when they are presented with a 'living will'. Such a lot depends on the responsible professional in charge of the patient. Professionals with knowledge and experience can intuit whether or not a patient can survive a crisis. They can even foretell whether that person might expect to be able to enjoy a reasonably good quality of life. Professionals cannot, however, guarantee to be right.

Medical decision-making also depends on the degree of trust patients, and/or their relatives, have in the physicians and surgeons upon whom they rely at such difficult moments in their lives. Throughout history good medical practice has depended upon patients' trust in their medical advisers. When trust is low, patients take matters into their own hands. They seek alternative therapies or make independent decisions about treatment. Patients who worry about the end point of their lives can make their desires known by living wills. When that end point comes, however, they may not be in a sufficiently healthy state of mind to confirm that decision themselves. That is where trust is important.

Living wills are popular. They may be hazardous for some patients. Some, when facing a crisis, may not know exactly what is best for them. Parliament is virtually the only institution in a democracy that can properly safeguard vulnerable people from exploitation. It remains to be seen if it agrees to legislation to make living wills binding in law.

Passive Euthanasia

Another concern among many older people who are alive today is the degree to which they will have to suffer in the process of dying. Many patients who ask to be 'put to sleep' are not so much talking about being killed as being taken out of their suffering. This may involve being rendered unconscious. Medical professionals can assure someone that they will do everything in their power to alleviate suffering, but they cannot guarantee success, especially in regard to mental suffering.

Horror stories that circulate among bystanders who know someone who has suffered, or is suffering, add to mental anguish among patients and relatives. So do media agencies that sell stories without due consideration for the victims whom they never see.

In countries like Britain, where active euthanasia is not legal, attitudes towards unrelieved suffering are changing. Many people, including professionals, now accept that giving patients drugs that relieve suffering, but may also shorten life, is desirable. All doctors faced with terminal illnesses, in which cure seems to be impossible, will strive to relieve suffering and ensure a dignified and pain-free death. In the majority of cases this is possible. In a few it is not. The margin between the intentional relief of pain and death from drugs to relieve that suffering is a narrow one. The same is true of other forms of suffering like suffocation. Most experienced medical doctors know their own minds. They manage to live their professional lives with a clear conscience that they have only intended to relieve suffering. They have not intended to kill.

Assisted Suicide and Active Euthanasia

Suicide itself is not a crime, and people who attempt to kill themselves are not punished if they survive. Many older and sick people do avail themselves of this solution to their suffering. The statistics show that in Britain more older men than women kill themselves each year. More women than men attempt suicide.[13] The incidence of suicide is highest in younger age groups. It is still too high among people who are over seventy-five years old, although the past decade has shown some reduction in overall numbers. By contrast, assisting someone to commit suicide is a crime. Patients may suffer from paralysing diseases that make their muscles too weak to take their own life. Some of them ask a relative or friend to help them to die. These are tragic situations involving prolonged suffering, sometimes slow suffocation. Those who assist someone to commit suicide are liable to prosecution for murder. In recent years, some people from Britain have taken relatives and friends overseas to countries where assisted suicide is legal.

Active Euthanasia

Active euthanasia is the deliberate taking of life at a patient's request. It is practised legally in some countries, notably Holland. In such countries a process of discernment takes place. There are consultations by patients and relatives with doctors. All must agree that the patient making the request is competent to make that decision. Once the patient expresses a firm and continuing desire for death, a date is set. A lethal injection is administered, usually in the presence of witnesses.[15] In these countries many medical doctors see this procedure as an extension of treatment and a compassionate response to need. For them it is a moral act. It is also sanctioned by law.

It might be thought that persons of religious faith would dissent from this viewpoint. They might believe that only God has the right to bestow life, and only God has the right to take life. Among some Christians, for instance, suffering is seen to have a purpose, even when it is extreme. They believe that God will bring good out of such suffering when it is willingly endured. However, attitudes, even among some Christian groups whose Churches offer strong condemnation of active euthanasia, are changing.[16]

Many Christians now maintain that God has given human beings wisdom to know the will of God, and the means to ensure a swift and merciful death. For them, too, active euthanasia is a moral act and one of great kindness to all concerned. They regard death as a benefit to those who choose it, but add that no one need choose this way of terminating life.

Active euthanasia presents society with some major problems. Pressure *can* be brought on doctors by patients and relatives. That makes the boundary between unintentional and intentional acts difficult to observe. Pressures *can* be brought on patients by relatives and friends, and sometimes by unscrupulous carers. These vulnerable patients may then request active euthanasia. The debate in countries, like Britain, that have not yet legalized active euthanasia is about patients' vulnerability to suggestion. It is also known that chronically ill patients are sometimes subjected to unscrupulous exploitation and misconduct among medical professionals.[17]

So far the discussion has centred on the desires of patients and relatives. There is, however, another factor at play in most postmodern societies. It is sometimes described as compassion. A section of society now considers that the quality of human life is more important than its persistence. People who think in this way argue that human life has no value unless the patient is conscious and capable of at least some autonomy. Pressure has been brought to bear on doctors to end life where a patient is in a 'persistent vegetative state' (PSV). Compassion is always cited as a reason for this request. Some professionals also support such action for economic reasons.

Persistent Vegetative States

A 'vegetative state' occurs when a patient's brain stem continues to function but there is no connection with the cerebral hemispheres. Such a patient is unconscious. The vital functions of respiration and heart beat continue to exist independently of mechanical intervention. Reflex movements of eyes, lips and muscles continue. Unless such a person's nutritional needs for water and food are adequately met, he or she will die. If such a person is sustained by being given food and water by artificial means, he or she may live for many years. Recovery of consciousness does not occur in patients who are in true 'vegetative states'. Any autonomy is impossible. Patients who live for long periods of time in a 'vegetative state' are described as being in a 'persistent vegetative state'.

At the outset of many accidents and illnesses of the brain it is impossible to tell whether or not the brain will recover sufficiently to allow the patient to regain consciousness and some independent living. So it is usual to treat all unconscious patients who are brought to hospital by the emergency services, vigorously. There is still hope of recovery. It is only later that it can be discovered that the patient is in an irreversible vegetative state.

This is one of the ethical dilemmas in modern technological medicine. Does human life have value per se? Does anyone at all have the right to deny food and water to someone who is still breathing, and whose heart is still beating? Is it cruel to deny death to such a person? Some will answer 'yes', some 'no'. The moral argument continues. Sometimes consensus is possible. Decisions *are* often made without recourse to legal judgments. When relatives disagree with professional doctors the case comes to court. Such occasions are always difficult, sometimes very painful. The recent cases of Anthony Bland[18] and Terri Schiavo[19] have made international headlines and led to much controversy.

Decisions about patients who are in a 'persistent vegetative state' are always difficult. Such decisions are usually made on the basis of trust between relatives and medical advisers. Where trust does not exist, terrible controversies may occur. The effect of such controversies is more widespread than the immediate families involved. It is not, therefore, surprising that many old people speak spontaneously of their fear of becoming 'vegetables'. Such dread destroys happiness in life's present gifts.

Brain Stem Death

Brain stem death is another feature of modern medical practice that worries older and younger people alike. There was a time when clinical death was assumed when a patient's heart and respiration stopped. Individual cells in bodily organs might remain alive for a time. It is well known, for instance, that hair continues to grow for some days after death. Those criteria of the cessation of respiration and circulation, however, were definitive for the whole person. They were pronounced dead. Nowadays, it is possible to sustain organ and cellular life by mechanical means. While machines keep respiration and heart rate going, the patient looks alive when they are not.

When a person's whole brain is dead it is electronically inactive. People who are 'brain dead' cannot survive on their own. They cannot live without mechanical aids to sustain respiration and circulation. Their bodily organs and tissues may remain alive by artificial means, but the moment those machines are turned off, circulation and respiration cease. The ethical difficulty here is to know just when brain death is certain. Only then can the machines be disconnected.

Medical professionals have put in many safeguards to ensure that machines are never turned off before at least two experienced doctors have certified that the brain is recording no activity. They do this by repeated electroencephalograms. Unfortunately, as has already been said, while the respiration and circulation are maintained artificially the patient looks alive, although they are not. This causes difficulty for relatives who cannot believe that the patient is dead. Some older people who hear about such cases, often from ill-informed sources, are worried by reports about such patients.

Such are the generally accepted medical facts about the end points of life. What of the human spirit? What might happen to that which gives personality its direction and helps it to relate? Does relationship depend on consciousness? At what moment does the human spirit become an entity that leaves the body; or does it? These questions are unanswerable except in rather anthropomorphic terms. Tentative answers to those questions, however, determine people's attitudes towards ethical issues at the end point of life. So they will be discussed in the next chapter.

8

Living Life to the Full to the Very End

Death must be distinguished from dying, with which it is often confused.

(Sidney Smith, 1771–1815)[1]

It hath often been said, that it is not death, but dying, which is terrible.

(Henry Fielding, 1707–54)[2]

Historical Attitudes towards Dying and Death

Death was commonplace in the eighteenth century when Henry Fielding and Sidney Smith were writing.[3] They wrote in the Age of Enlightenment[4] when medical science was beginning to take over from religion at the deathbed. Before the middle of the eighteenth century, people saw the whole of life from the moment of birth as a gradual process of dying. Death was the passage from earthly life to eternal life. European Papists and Protestants thought it mattered greatly how people lived their lives. Dying meant that a person was about to reach the summit of life through the gate of death. 'How a person died determined whether you went to heaven or hell.'[5] Those who were not yet old, or terminally ill, were constantly reminded that they were going to die. People generally died in the presence of family gatherings at the bedside and religious prayers and rituals.

Among Christians there was an art in dying. Roman Catholics hoped to die after they had confessed their sins. In this way they would be fortified by absolution and the 'last rites' of the Church. Those who died in a state of grace were fit for heaven. The state of Protestants' souls was already determined by whether or not they were converted Christians. Many Christians thought that sickness and dying were a well-deserved punishment for sin. Both were Job-like trials of faith. Anglicans and Protestants often took comfort from Bishop Jeremy Taylor's (1613–67) discourse on *Holy Dying*[6] and many other pious volumes of advice that were current at the time.

Ideas changed towards the middle of the seventeenth century. People like René Descartes (1594–1650)[7] and Galileo Galilei (1564–1642)[8] began to ask disturbing questions. Descartes' philosophy offered a mechanistic view of the human body. Galileo offered a different view of the relationship of the earth to the sun. Thomas Hobbes (1588–1679)[9] knew Galileo Galilei. He expanded Galileo's and Descartes' theories to include in his philosophy a mechanistic view of the universe and a materialistic view of the mind. At much the same time, Isaac Newton's (1642–727)[10] experimental natural philosophy and Antonie van Leeuwenhoek's (1632–1723)[11] microscopic discoveries were making their impact on medical practice. People's attitudes towards human life and death were rapidly changing.

God was no longer seen to be in absolute control of a person's life. Consequently, the care of the dying began to shift from families, friends and clerical pastors to physicians. It continued to do so in subsequent centuries.

Attitudes towards Dying and Death in the Twenty-first Century

In twenty-first-century developed countries dying is a process that may occur suddenly and naturally. Most people would consider that a happy way to die, although distressing for relatives and friends. Owing to advances in postmodern medicine, dying now often involves passing through a terminal phase of illness before a merciful death supervenes.

People alive today seldom see dying as a natural part of everyday life. It is rarely seen as the summit of life, or as a positive achievement. That statement needs some qualification. Scientists like Stephen Levine[12] have done much to help some patients, particularly in the United States of America, to think of dying as a process of birth. The focus of medical practice in industrialized societies has been to make dying as painless and anxiety free as possible. People with religious faith are welcome to ask for attention to their souls. The rest depend upon the medical, nursing and social work professions for assistance.

The discoveries of Lily Pincus, Elisabeth Kübler-Ross and Murray Parkes, pioneers in the understanding of the psychology of dying, are well known.[13] Cicely Saunders established the Hospice movement in Britain.[14] Hospices now exist throughout the world. Specialist doctors in palliative medicine and Macmillan nurses[15] bring their skills and expertise to people who are terminally ill. These people, and many others, have done much to alleviate physical and mental suffering during dying. Many books about dying are now available. A selection of these is included in the Some Useful Books section of this book.

The physical, mental and emotional aspects of dying are of the utmost spiritual importance, for the very core of personality is affected by what is happening to the whole of a person. This chapter will focus on older people's dying.

The Natural Process of Ageing and Dying

The death of older people is different from death in younger years, because it is expected. It is seen to be more appropriate than the death of younger people. Ideas about when a person is old enough to die vary greatly. On hearing of the death of someone aged between seventy and eighty years old, a friend a decade younger might say, 'Oh, quite young, wasn't she?' Personal experience of listening to many elderly people's opinions on these matters suggests that, in a country like Britain, people over eighty-five years old are considered to be ready for death. There is a certain excitement, however, if someone passes their ninetieth year. It is then thought a triumph to live until one hundred or more years have passed since birth.

Expecting to die, even wanting to die, is a feature of life after eighty-five. Contemporaries have died. The exigencies of technological life in the twenty-first century can be daunting. Elderly people increasingly feel out of tune with the speed of younger people's lives. A certain weariness overtakes the spirit. Increasing disability, loss of autonomy and the indignities of old age take their toll. People in later life sometimes suffer from economic hardship. They worry about the effect their needs are having on young relatives, friends and carers.

Few people nowadays are afraid of death. For people of all ages, dying is another matter. In the later years of life there is a *gradual* and natural change in the balance between the number of living, multiplying cells in the body and the number of cells that are dying, or have died. These cells are either no longer functional, or dead and irreplaceable. The body is running down gently. The person who is experiencing this gradual decline is scarcely aware of it unless vital organs begin to fail in a more rapid way. Healthy old people just go on living as well as they can. Muscles waste, joints ache, nothing works quite as well as it once did, but it is remarkable how people adjust. They become used to increasing disability, increasing general lethargy and increasing dependency on the help of others. This is true of those who are not afraid of old age and dying. Most people, however, are afraid of some aspects of dying.

Fears about the Physical Aspects of Dying

Fear is the single largest factor that interferes with the human spirit in later life. Throughout life people endure fear from time to time. They may worry about work, families and economic situations. They may suffer from debilitating or life-threatening illnesses. As people grow older they face more and different fears. Many have to worry about incontinence. Some dread their loss of autonomy. They do not know how they will manage the suffering and indignities that sometimes accompany dying. They are afraid of senility. They worry about living too long, about becoming a financial burden to their families. These are all natural fears. There are, however, two fears in particular that can afflict older people. Both of these have to do with moral and ethical issues that are current in our age.

Fears about Going into Hospital

Every time an older person goes into hospital there is an underlying fear that such a journey may be the last one he or she will make in this world. Going into hospital is always an intimation of mortality for a conscious person. It is pregnant with realism for older people. Hospital means going to a place that is strange. In hospital older patients have little or no control over what will happen to them. If they are very ill, there may be very little consultation with them when important decisions are being made. Going into hospital means leaving home. It means that other people will come into one's home. They will see one's personal effects, rummage in the drawers, invade one's privacy.

Small wonder it is, then, that so many people who reach eighty years of age begin to destroy letters. They throw out mementoes that have little meaning to anyone except themselves. They get rid of scruffy old garments that they love but others will not. They are doing this against the day when they will be taken to hospital. The word 'taken' is important: older people will sometimes resist that happening to them with a determination that veers on stubbornness. Such resistance is frequently inexplicable to younger relatives and friends: they are still seeing hospital as a place of healing. Elderly people do not always see it that way. Older people often dislike being 'taken' anywhere. They see being 'taken' to hospital, to a hospice, to a nursing home as 'the end'. It is an assault on the spirit. It signals the death of autonomy. It means that they are possibly near the end of their lives. They will only submit to this final loss of autonomy if they are too ill or too feeble to resist. Sometimes they will agree because they are afraid of upsetting people on whom they partly depend. They are afraid of what will happen to cherished relationships if they say 'no'.

When they express reluctance 'to go into hospital' older people are often expressing deeper fears that they cannot easily voice. Some alert elderly people will become acutely aware that they have made a 'living will'. They may fear it will be disregarded. Others may have made an 'enduring power of attorney'.[16] Suddenly, unaccountably, they worry about that complete loss of control over decision-making about their affairs. An 'enduring power of attorney' has to be made when the person making it is in a mentally competent state to do so. It enables a close relative, friend or solicitor to take over one's financial affairs should one become physically or mentally unable to manage them because of illness. A number of safeguards can be taken by the person who signs the document to ensure that their affairs are responsibly dealt with. Trust may exist at the time of signing. It may no longer exist when the time comes for the enduring power of attorney to be put into action. Legal advice is always necessary before making a decision to apply for a legal power of attorney.

Some elderly people make wills. Others do not. Again, their wills, or lack of wills, may cause great anxiety when time suddenly seems to be shorter than expected. Making a will is a highly spiritual act. Elderly people who are about to go into hospital often worry about whether or not they have made the right will. They may have forgotten what they have done. They may regret an element of vindictiveness that crept into the will they made some years ago. They may worry about leaving someone precious out of their will.

All these kinds of deep fears may surface at crisis times in older people's lives. They may underlie seeming obstinacy about 'going into hospital' or a nursing home. They are important. They are often neglected, however, because relatives and carers are afraid of raising such issues.

Fears about What Might Happen at the Hands of the Professionals in Hospital, Nursing Homes and Residential Care

People alive today live in a sophisticated society. Many will remain alert and able in mind when they reach eighty, or even ninety, years of age. Many will still be actively engaged in social life in their communities. They are the fortunate ones. Many, however, are not so blessed. Some of the less fortunate individuals in a modern industrialized society do remain ignorant of issues that surround death in a modern society. It may even be a blessing at this stage of life to be going gently into dementia. These people are unlikely to be worried about aspects of hospital life that may well worry their more able peers.

In hospital, mentally competent people are now usually asked whether they wish to be kept artificially alive if there is an acute life-threatening crisis. They may be asked about using heroic measures to prolong life at all costs. They might overhear a discussion about the use of drugs that suppress pain, but might shorten life. The media's widespread network of communication shares many details about important people's progress towards death. This has ensured that most people do know a great deal about what can happen to them when they are very ill. No wonder, then, that many elderly people are anxious when they need hospital treatment.

Who makes the judgement about whether it is worth being alive, or better dead? That question and the answer used to be left to God. It is not now. Now, human beings have immense power over life and death. No one can be trusted to use that power with the absolute assurance that he or she has the 'mind of God'; not even judges. Human beings alive today are living in a time of relativism, where scientific and medical knowledge far exceeds people's moral maturity and wisdom.

This area of older people's lives has nothing to do with fears about what may happen after death. No, it is to do with what may happen at the hands of other people. Some people are so afraid about what other human beings might do that they try to retain their autonomy by making 'living wills' ahead of time. Some decide to take their lives before they get to that stage of life at all. Horror stories in the media about what can, and does, happen to other elderly people grip some older people with apprehension. The truth is that people cannot foretell what is going to happen to them once they get 'carted off to hospital', as the following story shows.

'Martha' was a lively woman with a strong personality. In her late seventies she asked not to be resuscitated if she had an illness that would leave her brain-damaged if she did not die. Shortly after this, she had a 'stroke', and became unconscious. She was taken off to hospital in an emergency ambulance. Her daughter went with her. When they reached the emergency department the mother was still unconscious. Her daughter knew about her mother's wishes. She was hit by the thought, 'What if we get it wrong?' So she told the doctor about her mother's desire, and added, 'But not if there is a chance that she might recover enough to enjoy life.'

Poor young doctor! Who could possibly tell at that stage of the illness? As it happened he never had to make any decision. 'Martha' recovered consciousness and lived for several more years. From that point on, however, fear continued to haunt mother and daughter. In the mother's final weeks of life, she was dying from respiratory failure. It was not a pleasant way to die. She repeatedly begged for death to come. Then one day, when she was about to be given an injection, she fiercely and in a loud, and obviously frightened voice, said to the nurse, 'You're not going to kill me are you?'

'No,' the nurse replied, 'I am just giving you this injection to help your breathing.' It was a true statement. 'Martha' died an hour later.

The thoughts and feelings that people have when they still have control over their decisions may not be the same when they have lost their autonomy, but are still sane. Which nurse or doctor can ever be sure of their motivation when they give medication that will certainly alleviate symptoms, but might also induce death?

Doctors, patients and relatives are constantly facing scenes like this one. They are facing it in a culture where death is seen to be preventable, and life *can* be prolonged. Moreover, it is a culture in which 'authority' of any kind is open to challenge. When anything goes wrong in such a culture, it has to be someone's fault. Doctors are seen as cruel if they allow any suffering at all, even for the sake of prolonging life. They may be thought cruel if they give medications that have 'double effect' and so may kill the patient. Older people's beliefs and fears about what might happen to them at the hands of other people are real. They should be taken into account by all those who have concern for them.

Fears about other people are not confined to hospital personnel. Impatient relatives and carers can hurt elderly people through repeated verbal abuse, and sometimes through physical violence. Vulnerable older people *are* sometimes battered. They can be intimidated by threats. They can become paranoid and think that everyone is against them when the reverse is true. Becoming old, ill and highly vulnerable is no fun. It calls for understanding, empathy and patience among carers. Carers deserve sufficient respite from day-after-day caring to ensure those qualities can be preserved.

Fears about Judgement

The second great fear that can afflict older people has to do with judgement. Most elderly people alive today were born at a time when fear of the consequences of their actions was a guiding factor in their lives. The climate of the environment in which they grew up was a moral one. They may not have been born into a predominantly Christian culture. Nevertheless, the laws of any European or American country were based in the Judaeo-Christian tradition and on Graeco-Romano culture. Older people grew up knowing that actions that transgressed the law would be punished. People still are punished *if* they are caught. However, the laws of the country were not the only guiding principles that made old people conform when they were young. There was also a very strong code of moral behaviour by which they were judged by their elders, peers and local communities. Consequently, they acquired a sense of guilt if they acted against the code.

During any one person's lifetime the laws of the land and codes of moral behaviour change. When laws are manifestly unjust these changes are preferable to the outgoing laws. The past century has seen a lot of changes in society. It seems that laws have generally become more just, more compassionate. Legislators have often shown more common sense and compassion towards moral offenders than the populace. However, the pendulum may have swung too far. The decline of religious influence in a technologically sophisticated country *has* resulted in a high degree of individualism and intolerance of other people's ways of life. As a result those who disagree with such changes have become more intolerant.[17]

Today, some of the so-called civilized societies seem to have lost their way. In most heavily industrialized societies, especially in Europe and in the Americas, people now live in a culture where individual desires take precedence over the common good. They also live in a culture that suggests that they are never to blame for any misfortune that befalls them. Since so many people no longer believe in God, they cannot blame God. Instead, they blame one another, anybody other than themselves. Such a 'culture of blame' blinds people to their own faults and failures. It encourages them to take revenge on those whom they judge to be guilty of offences. Litigation follows. Victims may make war on those whom they judge to be guilty of endangering their way of life. Those who are elderly may find themselves out of step with prevailing moral attitudes. They may even begin to feel guilty at being alive at all.

Guilt in People in Later Life

Guilt, however it arises, is not a pleasant sensation. Most people, certainly in childhood, prefer to avoid it by conformist behaviour. They try to please those with whom they live. It is important to be liked, to be praised. The word 'sorry' becomes a natural part of their conversation. Phrases like, 'Please forgive me', or, 'I won't do it again', fall easily from their lips. When older people who are alive today were born, the idea of individual responsibility within a family, community and society was common. The idea that society itself had a corporate moral identity was a familiar one. Transgression reaped punishment. It was unusual to appeal for clemency because of unfortunate circumstances of birth or environment. This means that today's older generations are often out of step with the younger generation. They feel guilty, whereas younger people would not feel that unpleasant emotion.

In later life, people's long-term memories are often better than their short-term ones. This means that many find they can remember far back into childhood. Events they had forgotten are sometimes vividly recalled. Such memories are not always pleasant. In older age people may be beset by guilt. They may feel a general sense of failure. They may experience deep regrets for long-since broken relationships. They may recall the suffering they have inflicted on other people during their lives. Fear of hellfire may not enter into it at all. It is just guilt. They themselves are the judges of their behaviour, of the way they have lived their lives.

Guilt in people's older years is one of the saddest features about living for a very long time. Often it is too late to put things right. Attempts at reconciliation with estranged relatives or friends may fail. Loneliness and depression may prevail. All these emotions may become more overwhelming in the last months and years of people's lives.

Guilt among People who are Near the End of their Lives

Anxiety, guilt and depression were discussed in Chapter 2 as well as in this chapter. Guilty feelings at the very end of life may show themselves in somewhat different ways. Some guilty feelings may be justified. Many 'hauntings' of guilt, however, happen because of depression, more so than is apparent from the statistics of suicide. Chronic depression is common among people in later life. It may not be noticed because so many other things are happening at the same time. Physical and social needs take priority.

The human spirit, the core of personhood, suffers greatly when guilt besets it. Guilt that is the result of depression can sometimes be detected when the feelings are out of proportion to the crimes, errors and hurts being expressed. If real or pathological guilt persists, it may cause unspoken suffering. A general feeling of being a nuisance to those who care for them may begin to nag at such elderly persons. They may begin to feel that they *are* a burden to their families and friends. They worry that they will not be able to leave money to their children. They worry because their relatives, or carers, are so tired. In the end, elderly people may long for death as a way of escaping from the guilt of being alive. Suicide is not too easy to arrange when individuals are very old. General apathy towards life begins to take over their waking hours. Very elderly people may fall asleep as a way of escaping consciousness. Such behaviour may be attributed to natural old age.

After their eightieth birthday many people become acutely aware of their mortality. That is why they so often begin to re-experience old guilt. Guilt is so unpleasant that most people look for ways to banish it. Some individuals simply suppress guilt. They declare that they have never acted in ways that are harmful to their families and friends. They have never been in trouble at work or in the community. They contrast modern ways with their own ways of thinking and living. They may even trumpet their opinions about anything and everything to anyone who will listen. They lament the past. They refuse to change their opinions. Going on the offensive is a marvellous way of defending internal murmurs of conscience. Truth to tell, grumbling keeps many an elderly person happy and thriving.

Some older people do try to adapt to the prevailing climate of morality. Others try to come to terms with past mistakes and hurts. Many people just sit back and watch the world go by.

It seems to have less and less to do with them and, in any case, they become aware that they have a limited future. At this stage of life, however, many older people return to the great questions they asked when they were younger. 'What is going to happen when I die?' There is no answer to that question, of course. In a century or two's time, it may be quite irrelevant to the majority of people who will then be alive. It is not irrelevant to many old people who are alive today.

Fears about What Might Happen after Death

Ideas about ultimate destiny and God's judgement still abound among many elderly people who had moral and religious teaching when they were young. These ideas may well surface when human beings are on the verge of dying, or death.

In clinical medical and pastoral practice there seems to be a remarkable reluctance to raise this issue of ultimate judgement with elderly people. Some relatives, friends and carers pretend to optimism long after it is realistic to do so. When they do discuss what will happen after the elderly person dies, they tend to focus on practical matters. They may ask what the old person wants done with his or her possessions. They may discuss what hymns she or he would like at the funeral. They may utter platitudes about the 'afterlife', some of which are manifestly absurd by present-day rational standards. If professional carers and families do only that, they may deny elderly or dying individuals opportunity to voice their fears about their ultimate destiny. It is dangerous to assume that people who have always gone to church, or attended synagogue, will believe all that their faith professes. That cannot be taken for granted. There *are* ways of encouraging very old, terminally ill and dying patients to discuss their thoughts about their future in ways that are not intrusive or cruel. It is to be hoped that in future this will happen more than it apparently does at present.

Fear during the Terminal Stages of Life

People's fear about what will happen after they die sometimes becomes very clear during terminal illness. It may be assumed that the dying person would like the comfort of a visit from the local minister of religion. Such a visit, if not requested directly by the sick person, may cause great distress. On the other hand, declared atheists may find themselves wanting the ministry of someone who does have religious faith. This time of life requires great delicacy from carers.

It is not sensible to make rules that apply to everyone, irrespective of circumstances. The following story illustrates the need for some flexibility, even of good rules that protect patients from unwarranted attentions. In one of the cottage hospitals known to the present author, the rule was that the chaplain could not approach a dying person unless that person, or the close relatives, asked for such ministry. The chaplain was scrupulously careful to observe that rule. Nevertheless, it made life awkward, both for him and for the patients in the ward. His approach to any particular bed meant that the patient was an observant Christian. Word quickly went round the wards that a visit from the hospital chaplain meant that the person was likely to die. That was not necessarily true, but it led to some embarrassment among those who were pleased to see him.

The chaplain smiled at everyone, indulged in light-hearted general banter on his way to the persons he was visiting officially. Sometimes he casually stopped by another patient in an unthreatening way. Week after week, he passed by the bed of a declared atheist, 'Tom'. Tom had told the nurses he never wanted to see 'that God man', even on his deathbed. Tom was very ill and likely to die.

One night, at about eleven o'clock, the chaplain had a call from a very busy nurse. The hospital in question was a splendid one. Nurses often sat with their dying patients who had no relatives. When he arrived the charge nurse said, 'We're very short of staff tonight, and I've no one to sit with Tom: he's restless and seems frightened. Will you come and help us out?'

The chaplain, having heard about Tom's atheism, hesitated. 'He asked for you by name,' she said. 'He says he wants you to come.' Tom and the chaplain sat silently through the long night, just holding hands. 'Tom' murmured only a few words. He knew that the chaplain was praying silently. In the early hours of the next morning he died.

No one can know what changed Tom's mind, but, change his mind he did. The chaplain had ceased to be a threat to his peace of mind about himself, maybe because his need of human comfort at the hour of his death overrode his strong beliefs.

A single incident cannot lead to a generalization. This true story has been told because it is pertinent to any discussion about rules of behaviour in regard to older people who are dying. Good pastoral practice is different from general rules. Hard and fast rules of conduct are blunt instruments when it comes to individuals who are facing death. Society needs to find better solutions to the spiritual needs of human beings.

Meeting People's Spiritual Needs at the End of Life

Fears about dying, fears about judgement, are areas of real need when people are near to death. Open discussion, sensitive empathy and reassurance also need to be offered to relatives and friends. When one human being really meets another with empathy they can sometimes enable an older or sick person to say what is really on their mind. When a pastor is content to listen to patient and relatives without condemnation, there is the possibility of real healing. Carers are rightly happy when anyone attains to the peace of mind that enables them to die peacefully.

The spiritual needs of people of religious faith should always be taken into account by those who care for them. Any visit or religious ritual that seems appropriate to a dying person, or their relatives, *is* appropriate. Hospital and nursing home staff, even those without belief, are generally trained to send for Roman Catholic priests when Roman Catholic patients are dying. They often do not seem to think of doing such a thing for persons from other denominations. Anglican and Nonconformist hospital chaplains have often complained about this failure to send for them They are often told that the person in question was semi-conscious or unconscious. It is as if the nurses or relatives thought that prayer was useless unless it was audible. That is not so for people of religious faith. A pastor's absence may deny the believer of valuable strengthening on their last journey. This is the time when unspoken guilt or fear may be present, even though it cannot be articulated. Restlessness, crying, whimpering, incomprehensible muttering, may suggest to discerning carers that spiritual help is needed. Experienced pastors know this. They know the comfort that a trained person can offer in such situations. They also know from experience that such deep fears can sometimes be assuaged by touch and prayer, even though the dying person may be semi-conscious, or unconscious.

Pressure should never be brought to bear on people of declared religious belief that might override their real wishes. Similarly, pressure should not be brought on lapsed members of a religious faith to conform to expectation. This is a very sensitive area of ministry and one that calls for much tact and wisdom.

9

Life after Death

Since I am comming to that Holy roome,
Where, with thy Quire of Saints for evermore,
I shall be made thy Musique; As I come
I tune that Instrument here at the dore,
And what I must do then, thinke here before.
(John Donne, 1572–1631)[1]

Death was no stranger to the seventeenth-century poets like
John Donne. When he was only four years old his father died.
His first stepfather died when he was only sixteen years old. The
plague raged during his adolescent years. He would have grown
up in that climate of frequent death. Apart from the plague,
death was commonplace. His brother, his wife and two of his
children died before he became a priest in the Church of
England. His wife, Anne More, had borne him twelve children
of whom seven in all survived into adult life. She died shortly
after giving birth to a stillborn child. She was only thirty-three
years old. Four years later Donne became the Dean of St Paul's.
Prosperity and growing respect did not assuage his grief. His last
years were marked by sickness. Death haunted him. It dominated his poems. The poem that heads this chapter was probably
written in 1623 at a time when again the Plague was rife in
London.[2] It was certainly written during one of his bouts of
severe illness. Throughout his last years Donne meditated upon
death with a somewhat troubled spirit and in quite an obsessive
way. Indeed, he was so preoccupied with death that he dressed

up in his knotted shroud for his final portrait. He had the picture placed by his bedside so that he could ponder its meaning during his dying. The rictus on his lips makes it a grim portrait. It was the precursor of the effigy of him that now stands in St Paul's Cathedral in London.

At the time of his dying Donne was a realist. Death would signal the end of his fears whatever might happen. During his lifetime he had thought long and hard about the possibility of total annihilation at death. He had mused upon what would happen if God rejected him. 'Then,' Donne said, 'God might let my soul fall out of his hand into a bottomless pit, and roll an unremoveable stone upon it and leave it to that which he finds there.'[3] Towards the end of his life he appears to have changed. James Winny,[4] a Canadian writer on Donne, says that in his last illness the poet-priest was looking forward to the time of his dissolution. Winny comments, 'Death had been the king of terrors for Donne too; but the dead were beyond the reach of such fears.'[5]

Human Attitudes towards Death in the Twenty-first Century

Life in the twenty-first century is very different from that of the seventeenth century. Yet it is still true that people's beliefs about what happens to them after death colour their lives, especially among the very old.

Many people in society do not like thinking about death. Death is something that happens to other people. It happens in a sanitized way in hospital, in a nursing home, in a hospice, that is, a place that is hidden from most people's eyes. Most older people hope to die either suddenly, without any fuss, or in their own homes, in their own beds. They know, however, if they live in sheltered accommodation or residential homes, that will be unlikely.

Young people sometimes avoid the subject of death. They do not often think about the end of life unless some catastrophe happens to a close contemporary or relative. Then sometimes they connect that death with their mortality. People of all faiths take death more seriously as they get older. They do think about it from time to time, but it is painful. People who live in a highly materialistic, scientific culture find it difficult to believe in the continuation of the human personality in some form, or other, beyond death.

Belief about what happens to them after death will colour the way people want to die, the way they approach their dying. A confirmed atheist may live for the pleasure of life itself. Death is final. It is the end of them, the end of their personalities. People who are agnostic about the existence of God may not believe in personal survival. They may, and sometimes do, entrust their futures to God. Many decide not to worry about what happens after death. Death itself is a friend, not an enemy. Dying is what concerns them.

Attitudes towards Life after Death among Mainstream Ancient Religions

Hindus and Buddhists believe that finality of existence is a blessing that comes with perfect being. When they attain that state they need not return unless they choose to do so. Until then people's future lives depend largely upon how they have lived their present lives.

Hindus who die before they are perfect will be born again into another life. That life will take them into a higher state of being, or into a lower one. Living life well, according to Hindu scriptures, is what is important, and so is dying well. Absorption into Atman will not take place until the soul is at one with its Source. Even then the perfect soul may choose to return to earth as a reincarnation to show the way to people who are alive and seeking their own 'dharma'.[6] Buddhists do not need to believe in God,[7] but they do believe that the human spirit will go through cycles of reincarnation until it is perfect enough to be absorbed into infinity.

Ancient Egyptians mingled living experiences with a belief in immortality. They had elaborate burial chambers in which they placed the dead person. Food, drink and some possessions were put into the tomb to sustain the dead on their journey into the shadowy land of the next life.[8] Sometimes they slaughtered spouses and servants so that their souls might care for an important person in the afterlife.

Attitudes towards Life after Death among Members of Monotheistic Religions

The great monotheistic religions arrive on the stage of history comparatively late. Judaism, Christianity and Islam are all young faiths compared to the older ones. In these faiths, as taught by their orthodox exponents, reincarnation is not an issue. This life is all there is; how one lives it determines what happens after death. Reincarnation is, however, a tenet held by Kabbalists, some of the Hasidim and some unorthodox Christians.[9]

Orthodox Jews accept death as natural. Killing is viewed with abhorrence. Suicide, active euthanasia and murder are all condemned. Some Reform Jews do not view suicide or active euthanasia with such distaste.[10] From the time when they came under Greek influence until the Middle Ages, the dominant branches of the Jewish faith believed in the resurrection of the soul.[11] One strand of Jewish thought teaches that the souls of the dead return to the garden of Eden. They will wait there until after the Messiah has come, and the day of the general resurrection happens. They will then be reunited with their bodies. They will be judged and enter a period known as the Coming Age.[12] This is why Orthodox Jews do not cremate their dead. This custom is not now always observed. Maimonides (1137–1204),[13] however, taught that the resurrected body will eventually die. Only the soul can be considered to be immortal. Teachers who follow him, and Reform Jews, do not stress bodily resurrection. They do believe in the immortality of the soul. They dislike dogmatic statements and might, perhaps, follow Maimonides when he says:

It is in fact ignorance, or a kind of madness, to weary our minds with striving to discover things which are beyond our reach.[14]

Where possible dying Jews are accompanied by their close family and friends. When observant Jews know that they are dying they often recite this prayer:

I acknowledge before you, Lord my God, and God of my ancestors, that both my cure and my death is in your hands. May it be your will to send me a perfect healing. Yet, if my death is fully determined by you, I will lovingly accept it from your hand. May my death be an atonement for all the sins, iniquities and transgressions that I have committed before you. Make known to me the path of life: in your presence is fullness of joy; at your right hand bliss for evermore.[15]

They are not left alone and the opening words of the Shema[16] are recited as death comes close. Mourning rituals usually follow death. Although they are not of prime concern here, there are three stages of mourning. The Shiva is the first seven days after death. The Shloshim is the thirty days after the funeral. The Kaddish is recited on the anniversary of death. These three stages of mourning are well known among Jews.[17]

Among Christians there are a wide variety of opinions. The Anglican Creeds, as used in Britain, demonstrate this. The 1662 Prayer Book Apostolic Creed states: 'I believe in the resurrection of the body and the life everlasting.'[18] The Nicene Creed puts it differently: 'I look for the resurrection of the dead, And the life of the world to come.'[19] In *Common Worship*, now widely used in the Church of England,[20] the subtle differences are repeated. This gives some latitude for nuances of belief, at least among Anglicans. The problem about what happens to people after their deaths, however, is still present. This is partly the result of attitude changes and conflicts about the 'soul' during Anglican Church history.

Aristotelian philosophy and methodology undergirded much traditional Christian theology until the late nineteenth century. Aristotle saw the heart as the seat of soul.[21] The heart was the source of movement and sensation. He disagreed with his master, Plato, who thought that soul and body were distinct entities. These ideas still dominate some groups of Christians alive today.

Some Christians are still influenced by Cartesian dualism.[22] They think that the soul and body are distinct entities that separate from one another at death. Many Christians still believe that the soul flies out of the body at death. Some Christians believe that the personality survives death. Other Christians would say that the death of the brain includes death of the whole person, body, mind and spirit. The person is absorbed into eternal life in a different way. There is a complete death: 'What is sown is perishable.' The new resurrection body that is raised 'is imperishable'.[23] The mode by which this happens would be considered to be a mystery that could only be properly apprehended by faith.

Christian leaders and teachers seem to be united in their statements that the Christian religion does not teach that the soul is immortal. It does teach that eternal life is the destiny of the soul. It is, however, difficult to get those ideas coherently conveyed today. The prevailing culture is one in which ideas about immortality and reincarnation mix happily with 'reunion with loved ones after death' and vague agnosticism.

A number of Christians who profess the existence of God, the divinity of Christ and the resurrection of his body, believe that they are already living in resurrection life. Their personalities, their human spirits, are linked to God. They already have their identity in God's eternal love. They will continue to have identity in that love after death. At death they will be absorbed into God's love and God's purposes for creation. They will continue to contribute to the future of all creation as it moves towards a final consummation. Then there will be a general resurrection and a 'last judgement'.

Among people of the Muslim faith the soul (*ruh*) of human beings is located in the spiritual heart (*qalb*). Heart and soul make up the spiritual nature of humankind. Human bodies are the seat of animal nature (*ruh haywani*). They are sometimes driven by animal passions like anger and desire. The soul is the seat of God nature, the divine spark given by God to Adam and Eve, and given to all Muslims as their inheritance. The divine spark is independent of the body. It is untouchable, but infinite. Death is a taking off of the body, a letting of the soul fly to its Source providing that it is cleansed. Martyrdom obliterates all sins and brings with it the gift of the instant attainment of heaven.[24]

All these theories are current among multifaith communities. They are inexplicable to atheists. Atheists believe there is no God, no Source of creation other than an accidental conjunction of atoms. Many religious ideas are mysterious to agnostics. They simply say they do not know whether or not there is a God. They are equally mysterious to the 'death of God' adherents.[25] These people, who were prominent in the middle of the last century, believe there was a Creator God. He decided to die and leave the world with a legacy by which they could choose to live a God-like life if they wished. For them, too, death is the end of life.

The Importance of Ideas about Life after Death to People who are Dying

Patients do not generally mind whether their beliefs are Orthodox. It does, however, matter that those around them when they are dying take them seriously. It is, therefore, important that those who care for very sick and aged people should tactfully ascertain the opinions and wishes of their patients.

Hospitals and hospices have made progress in treating dying people with respect and due consideration for their dignity as human beings. Good pastoral care of that kind is only available to relatively few people in society. Patients who do not request spiritual care are unlikely to be visited by a pastor of faith. Hospital chaplains are no longer as free as they once were to walk round wards talking to everyone. Anglican chaplains used to have admission lists that included a note on denominational faith. They seldom do now. They rely on the patients and local clergy to ask for a visit. Older patients find this difficult. In the 'old days' patients saw chaplains talking to everyone. That happens less often nowadays. The argument against it goes like this: 'A visit from the chaplain may bode ill. Very few people are now religious. A visit from the chaplain may be intrusive on the patients' privacy.'[26] Exceptions are generally made for Roman Catholic patients because generations of nurses have been taught that patients of this denomination need the last rites if they are to be assured of their salvation.[27]

These postmodern attitudes in medical practice towards the religious beliefs of people have left many patients without support at the time when they most need it. Dying is one of the most important events of living. Frank discussion can be creative at such times. It can break through the conspiracy of silence that can be oppressive for dying people and their carers alike. It may not be appropriate in all cases, but the possibility of such a conversation should always be carefully considered. It should not necessarily be left to the patient to raise.[28]

Preparation for Dying

Human beings need to be able to look back over their lives. They sometimes need to be able to express sorrow for certain missed opportunities, or mistaken decisions and actions. More than that: the human spirit needs to be nourished by recalling past joys. These are all human needs. They are activities of the human spirit. They do not apply only to those who believe in judgement after death. This is something that many older people know instinctively. They often love to talk about the past. They are disappointed when they appear to bore other people. A small child loves to hear, and repeat, the same phrases many times. He or she will want bedtime stories repeated again and again. Woe betide a sleepy parent who tries to shorten the story. That is how children learn the language of life. It is how they apply what they hear to how they are becoming as they grow into a more mature childhood. Similarly, older people need to hear their own stories again and again, and they need to tell them. That is their way of preparing for death and the possibility, either of extinction, or of eternal life. It is their legacy to the future of humankind. Some few write for posterity, or leave a legacy of creative art behind them. Most do not. What they have to hand on to their families and friends are memories. It is cruel to deny them that opportunity, especially when they do not remember that they have told their stories before, and so repeat them.

'Memory boxes', collections of special memorabilia, have already been mentioned in Chapter 3. That is an excellent way of looking back on the past. It brings back sorrowful memories, but also joyful ones, especially during the younger part of older age. In very old age it is more helpful for family and friends to prompt memories, particularly when those memories revive times of shared pleasure with spouses and children.

Preparation for death is one of the most important phases of life and it has to begin long before people are dying. Some great Christians, like Bishop John Robinson[29] and Donald Nicholl,[30] have written about their attitudes towards death. These writings can be helpful to those who are thinking about their own death. They can also be counter-productive; the reader might know that she or he would be unlikely to meet death with such serenity. Happy the old person who has friends or carers who will take the time to get to know the old person's past. They may, perhaps, have shared that past. If they have not, they will at least take the trouble to listen. This is not common practice in postmodern society. Friends sometimes express surprise at funerals: 'I never knew that', or, 'She kept herself to herself'.[31] A lifetime's 'being' who you are deserves better than that. It merits more than a fifteen-minute funeral taken by someone who has never heard of the person at all.

When older people know that they are near to death, but are still conscious, carers should work within the framework of the moral and spiritual beliefs of the old person. There is no point in beginning to argue with them. They do not need to be converted to better ways of thinking. They do not even need a return to the faith of their childhood unless, of course, they want to do that.

People of the older generations alive today will include some who are afraid of hell. That fear should be recognized. If possible it should be assuaged by calm words and by touch. The comfort of touch and embrace need not be denied to a dying person, as was said in Chapter 8. Touch conveys more than words can do about the solidarity between human beings. It is a truly spiritual work of mercy.

Relatives and close friends are an essential part of old people's thoughts. A few people are friendless. Kind carers in the community, or sympathetic nurses in hospital, are treasured by some of them. Dying patients need to talk about the people they love, even if, at the same time, they sometimes hate them. They need to reassure themselves about the future of those who will live on when they are dead. Some older people can only manage dying because they believe that they 'live on through their children'. That is the afterlife for them. Their genes are in future generations; their children and grandchildren are their future. Families and friends who deny such conversations may ease themselves from anticipatory grief, but they may add to the pain of a terminally ill or very old person.

Finally, it needs to be said that the human spirit is not coterminous with full consciousness. Hearing is the last of the senses to disappear before death. Those who are dying can sometimes hear what is said around them. They may overhear what is said about their death, even what is said about their funerals. Tests in comatose patients have demonstrated face recognition.[32] It is possible that the human spirit can communicate without sounds. Such at any rate is the belief of those who accompany dying patients in prayer, aloud or silently. Such ministry is precious. It should not be denied because a patient is beyond hearing. In a moving passage in Elizabeth Kübler-Ross's influential book *On Death and Dying* the author comments:

Those who have the strength and love to sit with a dying patient in the *silence that goes beyond words* will know that this moment is neither frightening nor painful, but a peaceful cessation of the functioning of the body. Watching a peaceful death of a human being reminds us of a falling star; or of a million lights in a vast sky that flares up for a brief moment only to disappear into the endless night for ever. To be a therapist to a dying patient makes us aware of the uniqueness of each individual in this sea of humanity. It makes us aware of our finiteness, our limited life span. Few of us live beyond our threescore years and ten and yet in that brief time most of us create and live a unique biography and weave ourselves into the fabric of human history.[33]

There speaks a great medical doctor whose pioneering work on the stages of dying has benefited countless patients throughout the world.

Ideas about life after death are important. No one can predict how they will react to the onset of death. Staunch believers cannot be certain that they will not be assailed by doubt. In the end, the journey through death is made alone. When John Donne was on his deathbed in 1631, he wrote his last poem, 'A Hymn to God the Father'. This is the last stanza:

> I have a sin of fear, that when I have spun
> My last thread I shall perish on the shore;
> Swear by thy self that at my death thy Sun
> Shall shine as it shines now, and heretofore;
> And having done that, thou hast done,
> I have no more.[34]

In some published versions of the poem the word Sun is spelt Son. Donne loved playing with words and often used them in ways that had a double meaning when said aloud. Such ambiguity is satisfying to the human spirit.

Afterword

I am a willing prisoner of hope.
(Desmond Tutu, 2005)

These words of Archbishop Desmond Tutu, made in another context, reflect my own attitude towards the later years of life. I have found those later years to be challenging, perhaps the most challenging years of a long life. A lifetime of learning and experience has resulted in memories and reflections about the past that are not always pleasant to meet in the present moments of later life. Like many people of my generation, I have wandered through those past memories with some unease. The 'what if' questions surface at times, despite knowing they can be unhelpful. The 'wish I hadn't' feelings of guilt surface in the long night hours. Having to face questions about the effect of my personal decisions and actions on other people's lives, especially those of my children and close family, have at times been tormenting. The frequent failures to live true to my beliefs have been distressing.

I have plenty to lament, yet remain a willing prisoner of hope. At the end of this book, I ask myself why? Why in the face of rigorous intellectual searching, doubt and much disappointment, do I remain a person of profound faith in the goodness of the human spirit? Why am I still hopeful for the human race?

I know that part of that hope has been fostered by the older people I met when I was a young person. They were the heroes and heroines that inspired me, led me on, encouraged me on the way. When I met them, or read about them, or learnt from their writings, their teachings often kept me going through periods of frustration and near despair. At this stage of my life, however, I want to testify that the greatest help during a long life has been the gift of trust that sometimes amounts to faith. Faith has taken me on a journey that was dominated in youth by fear of judgement. It has led me to an old age where I am happy to be imprisoned in hope and love.

When I was young I judged myself. I feared the judgement of other human beings. I judged other people. I have spent a lifetime pursuing God in and out of various Christian institutions. I have walked in the company of people of many faiths. The journey has brought me to a discovery of freedom and love that I could not have envisaged in my young and middle years of life. So I am thankful I have lived as long as I have done. I am grateful for the stresses and disappointments of youth and middle age. I am thankful for aches and pains of old age. Without stress and disappointment I never would have known what it was to struggle to preserve some ideals. Strong opposition to some of those ideals strengthened my desire to work for the betterment of humankind. I have lived long enough to glimpse a future that will be better for my successors than it was for my own generation when we were born. Without them I might die a pessimist about the nature of the human spirit. I am not a pessimist: nor am I an optimist. I do not look at human nature, my own or other people's, with rose-coloured spectacles. I cannot turn my back on a world to which I have contributed in negative, as well as in positive ways. Anger and rage about the way it has been, and is, in my own lifetime continue to spur me towards wanting it to be a better place for my successors.

Long ago, however, I allowed myself to be embraced by faith and hope and love. It is these three aspects of human experience that have defeated a tendency towards being judgemental. Despite some pretty horrific Church teaching in my youth, I have met a God who has taught me not to be judgemental towards myself. I have learnt not to be judgemental towards other people, however horrific their actions seem to me to be. In the end Judgement has to be left in the hands of God. What people alive today can do at this present moment is to encourage ourselves and others to hope. We need to trust in the goodness of the human spirit, made 'in the image of God'. We need to continue to love to the very end of life. So, yes, I am a 'willing prisoner of hope'.

References and Notes

Introduction

1 William Blake (1757–1827), 'To God', *Oxford Dictionary of Quotations (ODQ)* (2nd edn; London: OUP, 1953), p. 74:27.

2 H. F. Amiel, *Amiel's Journal* (London: Macmillan, 1918), p. 218.

3 La Jeunesse d'H. F. G. Amiel, http://www.amiel.org/atelier/oeuvre/editions/jeunesseamiel.htm, accessed June 2005.

4 Tristine Rainer, *Discovering Joy,* feature article on writer's work on Diary work, http://www.soulfulliving.com/discovering joy.htm, accessed 26 May 2005.

5 Alexander Pope (1688–1744), a poet of the Enlightenment, born in London at a time when Roman Catholics were persecuted. He was ill for most of his life and had spinal tuberculosis which gave him a humpback. Http://www.kirjasto.sci.fi/apope.htm, accessed 7 July 2005.

6 Alexander Pope, *An Essay on Man*, written in 1733–34. Its main theme is that human beings are part of nature's diversity of living forms. Reference as above, and quotation from Ep. ii, l.I, *ODQ*, p. 383:22.

7 Psalm 90.10, *Book of Common Prayer* (1662).

8 Constantine Petros Cavafy, Greek poet, born in Alexandria, raised in England and employed mainly in Egypt as an employee of the Irrigation Office. His complete works were only published after his death.

9 E. M. Forster (1879–1970). Noted English author and critic. A member of the Bloomsbury Group.

10 Constantine Petros Cavafy, 'Ithaca', in *The Complete Poems of*

Cavafy (trans. Rae Dalven; New York and London: Harcourt, Brace, Jovanovich, Inc., 1948), p. 36.

Chapter 1 Ageing and the Human Spirit

1 William Shakespeare, *As You Like It*, Act 2: scene 3.
2 Ibid., Act 2: scene 6.
3 Mortimer Collins (1827–76). Collins was a teacher, novelist and poet, who became an enthusiast for walking in the country. *Oxford Dictionary of Quotations*, p. 153:19.
4 Internet, Infoplease, *Infant Mortality and Life Expectancy for Selected Countries*, 2004, accessed 26 March 2005.
5 Ibid.
6 *Book of Common Prayer*, Psalm 90.10.
7 These attitudes, to a greater or lesser degree, of thinking that some people are 'superior' to others, or more deserving than others, underlie discriminatory attitudes towards peoples of different races, classes, genders and sexes. Taken to extremes they justify holocaust and genocide.
8 Imanuel Kant (1724–1804), *ODQ*, p. 282:5.
9 René Descartes (1596–1650), *ODQ*, p. 172:26.
10 William Shakespeare, *As You Like It*, Act 2: scene 7.
11 Shakespeare, *King Lear*, Act 5: scene 3.

Chapter 2 Meeting Some of the Challenges of Later Life

1 John O'Donohue, 'Spirituality as the Art of Real Presence', *The Way* Supplement, (London: Burns & Oates, 1998), p. 86.
2 John O'Donohue, *Anam Cara: A Book of Celtic Wisdom* (New York: HarperCollins, 1998).
3 Donohue, 'Spirituality', *The Way*, p. 86.
4 Ibid., p. 86.
5 Christina Rossetti, 'Up-hill', *ODQ*, p. 410:2.
6 O'Donohue, 'Spirituality', p. 86.
7 Dylan Thomas (1914–53), 'Elegy for a Dying Father', *Six Centuries of Verse* (selected and ed. Anthony Thwaite, London: Thames Methuen, 1984), p. 249.
8 St Joan's Alliance and the Christian Parity Group worked together with many other secular feminist organizations during the passage of the 1975 Sex Discrimination Act.

9 Julia Lawton, *The Dying Process: Patients' Experiences of Palliative Care* (London, New York: Routledge, 2000), pp. 175–6.

10 Sarah Woodward, 'Brain Power', *Cambridge University Alumni Magazine* (*CAM*), No. 44 (Lent 2005), p. 19.

11 See Chapter 8.

12 The Nun's Prayer, source unknown. This version printed by Tom Tilley Ltd., Bristol.

13 Ibid.

14 Joshua Kroll, my grandson, who has given me permission to use this account.

15 Age Concern. For the nearest centre please look in local Telephone Directory.

16 O'Donohue, 'Spirituality', p. 86.

17 Ibid., pp. 86–7.

Chapter 3 Living Life to the Full through Finding Freedom in Later Life

1 Lewis Carroll, *Alice in Wonderland*, Ch. 5.

2 University of the Third Age is a programme specially designed for older people. Branches are to be found in most towns and cities. They bring people together and keep older minds lively.

3 I first met 'memory boxes' through the Alzheimer course for 'buddies' that I went to in Wales. The Methodist Housing for the Aged has leaflets describing how to use them.

4 This refers to Sir Ralph Fiennes' experiences on an Everest expedition in July 2005. At first it seemed that he was going to push himself and his guides into danger. His wisdom in knowing when to stop, even when very high on the mountain, was impressive.

5 This refers to Abigail Witchalls whose spine was injured through a knife attack on 20 April 2005, and to all other quadriplegics and paraplegics who live life to the full despite severe physical disabilities.

6 Fr Cyril was profiled on *See Hear* on BBC 2 on 21 May 2005; information from the Internet accessed on http://www.bbc.co.uk/cgi-bin/education/betsie/parser.pl/0005/www.bbc.co.uk/seehear/.

7 John O'Donohue, 'Spirituality as the Art of Real Presence',

The Way Supplement (London: Burns & Oates, 1998), p. 86.

8 Mrs Dillys Lucas of Monmouth, Monmouthshire, Wales. She has given permission for this account of her later years of life.

9 Bert Jones, who lived in Monmouth. His relatives have given me permission to tell his story.

10 William Shakespeare, *King Lear*, Act v.3:viii.

11 Dame Felicitas Corrigan, OSB, *Helen Waddell* (London: Victor Gollancz Ltd, 1986). Helen Waddell was a noted scholar, translator and writer. She began to suffer from Alzheimer's disease when she was 55 years old, gradually but steadily deteriorated and died at the age of 76 on 5 March 1965.

12 John Bayley, *Iris*, and *Iris and the Friends* (London: Duckworth, 1998). Iris Murdoch was an eminent philosopher who also wrote many very well-known novels. She too suffered from Alzheimer's disease and its terrible progress was documented by her husband, John Bayley, and in the film, *Iris*.

13 Brother Lawrence, *The Practice of the Presence of God* (London: A. R. Mowbray Ltd, 1977).

14 Jean Pierre de Caussade (1675–1751) *Abandonment to Divine Providence (1741)* (French edition, H. Ramière, 1867; English translation by John Chapman, 1921). De Caussade was a Jesuit writing at the time of the Quietist controversy when mysticism was under attack. His writings did much to restore the good reputation of this kind of prayer.

15 Nelson Mandela (1918–). Imprisoned in South Africa, 1964–90; Nobel Peace Prize, 1993; first black president of South Africa, 1994–99.

16 Desmond Tutu, Archbishop (1931–). Anti-apartheid Christian leader in South Africa; Nobel Peace Prize, 1984.

17 Desmond Tutu speaking on the *David Frost Show*, BBC 1, 29 April 2005.

18 Dame Felicitas Corrigan, *Helen Waddell*, p. 348.

Chapter 4 Relationships in Later Life

1 Paul Tournier, *The Seasons of Life* (London: SCM Press, 1964), p. 23.

2 Fritjof Capra, *The Tao of Physics* (Wildwood House, 1975, and Fontana, 1976). Capra is an Austrian-born physicist in the USA. This book is about the relationship between modern

physics and Eastern mysticism. It includes explanations of particle/wave theories of matter.

3 Dame Jane Goodall went to live among chimpanzee families at Gombe in 1961. Her observations on chimpanzee behaviour led to many publications, a PhD in 1965 and some films for the National Geographic Magazine.

4 Michael Neugebauer, photograph taken at JGI Sweetwaters Chimpanzee Sanctuary, 2000, published in *Cambridge Alumni Magazine*, No. 44 (Lent 2005), p. 10.

5 Michael Leech, *Great Apes, Our Face* (London: Blandford Press, 1996).

6 John Donne, 'Devotions', *ODQ*, p. 186:27.

7 Carl Jung (1875–1961). Swiss psychiatrist, friend and colleague of Sigmund Freud. Jung broke away from Freud when he published *The Psychology of the Unconscious* in 1912. There is an informative article on *Carl Jung and the Collective Unconscious* on http://lcc.ctc.edu/faculty/dmccarthy/eng1204/seven-lecture.htm.

8 John O'Donohue, 'Spirituality as the Art of Real Presence', *The Way* Supplement (London: Burns & Oates. 1998), p. 86.

9 The Society of Psychical Research, founded 1882 by a group of distinguished Cambridge scholars. Conducts research and publishes findings in journal.

10 Iulia de Beausobre, *The Woman Who Could Not Die* (London: Chatto and Windus, 1938).

11 Iulia de Beausobre, *Creative Suffering* (London: Dacre Press, 1940). Now available from Fairacres Press, Fairacres, Oxford.

12 Julia Namier, *Lewis Namier* (Oxford: Oxford University Press, 1971).

13 Constance Babington-Smith, *Iulia de Beausobre* (London: Darton, Longman and Todd Ltd, 1983).

14 J. R. R. Tolkein, *The Lord of the Rings* (London: Allen & Unwin).

15 *Star Wars*. The first film in this genre. The character Obi-Wan Kenobi was played by the actor Alec Guinness.

16 J. K. Rowling, *Harry Potter* series.

17 David Wilkinson, 'Decision of Utter Madness', *The Times*, 29 March 2005.

Chapter 5 Caring for the Human Spirit of Older People

1 A. A. Milne, *Winnie the Pooh* (London: Methuen & Co, 1965), p. 90.
2 Francis Bacon, *Advancement of Learning* (1605), Bk I.i.3.
3 John O'Donohue, 'Spirituality as the Art of Real Presence', *The Way* Supplement (London: Burns & Oates, 1998), p. 86.
4 Peter Richards, 'Mirror of Humankind', *Cambridge Alumni Magazine*, No. 44, pp. 10–13.
5 Ibid., p. 11.
6 Edgar Adrian, quoted in P. Richards, 'All in the Mind', *CAM*, No. 44, p. 18.
7 Sarah Woodward, 'Brain Power', *CAM*, No. 44, p. 19.
8 Rita Carter, *Mapping the Mind* (London: Weidenfeld & Nicholson, 1992), pp. 13–4.
9 Joseph Addison, *Hymns Old & New* (Complete Anglican edn), No. 732.
10 Thomas Carlyle, *Heroes and Hero Worship; The Hero as Divinity*, quoted in *ODQ*, p. 126:22.
11 Rabbi Lionel Blue, '*Is There Anyone Else Up There?*', article published in *Mount Carmel* (July–Sept. 2002), *Review of the Spiritual Life*, Carmelite Priory, Boar's Hill, Oxford, OX1 5HB, p. 24.
12 *One Foot in the Grave*. Richard Wilson and Annette Crosbie took the leading roles. BBC productions.
13 Age Concern. See list of helpful organizations at end of book.
14 Crossroads. See Some Helpful Addresses at end of book.

Chapter 6 Making Choices in Later Life

1 Wisdom 2.4–5 (NSRV).
2 Deuteronomy 30.19–20 (NSRV).
3 Wisdom 2.3.
4 Robert Browning, 'Bishop Blougram's Apology', from selection by W. E. Williams, *The Penguin Poets* (London: Penguin, 1954), p. 225.
5 Ibid., p. 227.
6 Miguel Unamuno, quoted in Internet article, 'Books and Writers', http://www.kirjasto.sci.fi/unamuno.htm. Accessed 23 April 2005 (p. 3).
7 Psalm 41.9.

8 John O'Donohue, 'Spirituality as the Art of Real Presence', *The Way* Supplement (London: Burns & Oates, 1998), p. 86.

9 Internet, 'The Moral Status of Animals', *Stanford Encyclopaedia of Philosophy,* http://plato.stanford.edu/entries/moral-animal.

10 Ibid.

11 Ibid.

12 William Wordsworth (1770–1850), 'My Heart Leaps Up', *ODQ*, p. 577:25.

13 Reports in the *Daily Mail* and *The Times* newspapers, 5 May 2005.

14 The Disablement Act became law in 2005.

15 Age Concern – see Some Helpful Addresses.

16 Help the Aged – Some Helpful Addresses.

17 Betty Houghton of Hastings.

18 Peter Wilson of Monmouth.

19 Methodist Homes' Centre for the Spirituality of the Ageing – see Some Helpful Addresses.

20 Church Army – see Some Helpful Addresses.

21 *Psalm* – see Some Helpful Addresses.

22 Martin Thompson, 'Life Science', article about *Contact*: Student Community Action, *CAM* (Lent 2005), No. 44, p. 37.

23 Jonathan Conlin, 'Contact', *CAM* (Lent 2005), No. 44, p. 37.

Chapter 7 Some Ethical Issues of Later Life

1 Poster on the wall of Fairfield Hospital, Bury, Lancs, February 2005.

2 Olivier Clément, *On Human Being: A Spiritual Anthropology* (London and New York, New City Press, 1986 (French edn), 2000 (English edn)).

3 BBC News item, BBC 1, April 2005.

4 This refers to the possibility of proportional representation and devolution.

5 In 2005 the Post Office introduced a scheme to reward their employees for not going sick. It is said to have been pretty successful.

6 The abstention of the USA from the Kyoto protocol.

7 Thomas Malthus (1766–1834). Internet biographies: http://www.blupete.com/Literature/Biographies/Philosophy/Malthus.htm.

8 China has recently lifted its restriction on family limitation in some areas. Some families are now allowed two children.

9 Roy Porter, *The Greatest Benefit to Mankind, A Medical History of Humanity from Antiquity to the Present* (London: Fontana Press, 1997, p. 367).

10 Sam Lister and David Chester, *The Times*, 1 July 2005, p. 11.

11 Arthur Hugh Clough, 'The Latest Decalogue', *ODQ*, p. 146:35.

12 Living Wills. Internet Clickdocs, http://www.clickdocs.co.uk/glossary/living-will.htm, accessed 26 June 2005.

13 Ibid.

14 Internet: Suicide Statistics 1992–2002, http://www.befrienders.org/info/statistics.php, accessed 26 June 2005.

15 Personal communication from Dutch patient who asked for euthanasia in 2003.

16 Personal discussions with Christian groups, 2004–2005.

17 Harold Shipman was the most notorious of these professionals but he is by no means alone.

18 Internet – http://www.swansea-mrcgp.co.uk/Topics/euthanasia/withdrawing%20treatment.doc.

19 Michael Gove, 'A Nagging Sense of Injustice', *The Times*, 29 March 2005 and Jacqui Goddard, 'America World News', *The Times*, 29 March 2005.

Chapter 8 Living Life to the Full to the Very End

1 Sidney Smith, Revd (1771–1845), *ODQ*, p. 505:13.

2 Henry Fielding (1707–54), *Amelia*, Bk iii, Ch. 4, *ODQ*, p. 204:7.

3 Roy Porter, *The Greatest Benefit to Mankind* (London: Fontana Press, 1987, Ch. 10, on Enlightenment), p. 145.

4 Ibid., pp. 145–203.

5 Ibid., p. 214.

6 Jeremy Taylor, (1613–67), *Holy Dying* (1651), edited by P. G. Stanwood (Oxford: Oxford University Press, 1989).

7 Porter, *Greatest Benefit to Mankind*, pp. 217–19.

8 Ibid., p. 217.

9 Ibid., p. 219.

10 Ibid., p. 246.

11 Ibid., p. 204–26.

12 Stephen Levine, pioneer in helping people to think of death as a birth. Author of many books including *Guided Meditations, Explorations and Healings* (London: Gateway Press, 2000).

13 Elisabeth Kübler-Ross (1926–2004), *Death and Dying* (London: Routledge, 1997).

14 Cicely Saunders, OM, DBE, FRCP, FRCS (1918–2005). Founder of St Christopher's Hospice, Sydenham, London. Pioneer in palliative medicine.

15 Macmillan nurses are working in all towns in Britain and your family doctor will know how to find them.

16 Further information from http://www.oca.act.gov.au/attorney.

17 This refers to attitudes towards gay people in the ministry of the Anglican Church.

Chapter 9 Life after Death

1 John Donne, 'Hymn to God, my God, in my Sickness', *Penguin Book of Religious Verse*, introduced and edited by R.S. Thomas (Penguin Press, 1963), p. 33. This may have been written in 1623, during a bout of spotted fever, according to Walton, his first biographer, but manuscripts for this poem and for 'A Hymn to God my Father', were circulated together only in 1635.

2 James Winny, *A Preface to Donne* (London and New York: Longman Ltd., 1970, 1981), p. 35.

3 Ibid., p. 46.

4 James Winny, Professor of English Literature at Trent University, Peterborough, Ontario, Canada. He also taught at Cambridge and Leicester in England. *A Preface to Donne*, p. 46.

5 Ibid., p. 46.

6 'Dharma' – the ultimate law of all things. Buddhists try to live in accordance with these principles.

7 Zoë Sallis, *Ten Eternal Questions, Wisdom, Insight and Reflection for Life's Journey* (London: Duncan Baird, 2005), p. 33: direct quotation from His Holiness, the Dalai Lama.

8 Roy Porter, *The Greatest Benefit to Mankind* (London: Fontana Press, 1987)

9 Nicholas de Lange, *Introduction to Judaism* (Cambridge: Cam-

bridge University Press, 2000), pp. 151–3, and personal conversations with some Christian members of the Society of Psychical research.

10 Julia Neuberger, information from House of Lords and from an article on her new book, *The Moral State We're In*, in *The Independent* (6 March 2005), p. 9.
11 De Lange, *Introduction to Judaism*, p. 210.
12 Ibid.
13 Ibid., p. 211.
14 *The Wisdom of Israel* (London: Four Square Books, *New English Library*, 1962), p. 363.
15 De Lange, *Introduction to Judaism*, p. 115.
16 'Hear O Israel, The Lord is our God, The Lord is One.'
17 De Lange, *Introduction to Judaism*, p. 117.
18 *Book of Common Prayer*, 1662, Apostle's Creed at Matins.
19 *Book of Common Prayer*, 1662, Nicene Creed at Service of Holy Communion.
20 *Common Worship*, services of Matins and Eucharist.
21 Roy Porter, *The Greatest Benefit to Mankind* (London: Fontana Press, 1987), p. 65.
22 Ibid., pp. 217–19.
23 1 Corinthians 15.42–43, NRSV.
24 Robert Frager, *The Wisdom of Islam* (Alresford: Godsfield Press, 2002), pp. 95–9.
25 This was a movement, predominantly of the 1960s, associated with Nietzsche – 'God is dead', developed by Gabriel Vahanian, Thoms J. J. Altizer and Paul van Buren. Its influence waned in the late 1970s.
26 Personal experience as a hospital chaplain, 1990–2000.
27 Ibid.
28 Ibid.
29 John Robinson, quoted in Eric James, *A Life of Bishop John A. T. Robinson* (London: Collins, 1987).
30 Personal communication from Professor Donald Nicholl, author of *Holiness* (London: DLT, 1981). Also see article by him in *Tablet* (5 July 1997), 'My Last Voyage', http://www./thetablet.co.uk/cgi-nbin/register.cgi/tablet-00097.

31 Personal experience as a priest of the Anglican Church.
32 See Chapter 5, note 7.
33 Elizabeth Kübler-Ross, *On Death and Dying* (London: Routledge, 1997), pp. 246–7.
34 John Donne, 'A Hymn to God the Father', *ODQ*, p. 185:24.

Some Useful Books

This is not a comprehensive Bibliography. It consists of books that I have read myself and have found helpful. Each of the organizations mentioned in the addresses section has a list of its own publications. In addition there is a good Internet source, Catalogue of the Catholic Central Library, at the website http://www.catholic-library.org.uk.

General

Bytheway, Bill, *Ageism* (Maidenhead: Open University Press, 1995).

Farmer, Penelope (ed.), *The Virago Book of Grandmothers, An Autobiographical Anthology* (London: Virago Press, 2000).

Levine, Stephen, *Guided Meditations, Explorations and Healings* (London: Gateway Press, 2000).

Shoard, Marion, *The Daily Telegraph: A Survival Guide to Later Life: How to Stay Healthy, Happy, Mobile and in Control* (London: Constable & Robinson, 2004).

Waterhouse, Michael, S*taying Close, A Positive Approach to Dying and Bereavement* (London: Constable & Robinson, 2003).

Books about Spirituality and Ageing

Fischer, Kathleen, R., *Winter Grace: Spirituality and Ageing* (Nashville, TN: Upper Room Books, 1998).

Guenther, Margaret, *Towards Holy Ground, Spiritual Directions for the Second Half of Life* (Boston: Cowley Press, 1995).

Jewell, Albert (ed.), *Ageing, Spirituality and Well-being* (London and Philadelphia: Jessica Kingsley, 2004).

Leveson Centre (Temple Balsall) produces a comprehensive bibliography, *The Spiritual Needs of Older People: A Resource List*.

McKinley, Elizabeth, *The Spiritual Dimension of Ageing* (London and Philadelphia: Jessica Kingsley, 2001).

Simpson, Ray, *Before We Say Goodbye* (London: HarperCollins, 2002).

Snowdon, David, *Ageing with Grace – What the Nun Study Teaches us about Leading Longer, Healthier and More Meaningful Lives* (London: Fourth Estate, 2001).

Weaver, Andrew, SJ, *Reflections on Aging and Spiritual Growth* (Nashville, TN: Abingdon Press, 1998).

Some Helpful Addresses

General

Age Concern

This organization is concerned with all aspects of ageing. Has a research programme, **Age Concern Institute of Gerontology,** Kings College Hospital, Denmark Hill, London SE5 9RS.

Astral House
1268 London Road
London SW16 4ER
020 8765 7200
Website: http://www.ageconcern.org.uk

Alzheimer's Society

This organization is nationwide. Works for people who have dementia and for their families. Has extensive research, a regular newsletter and locally organized groups.

Gordon House
10 Greencoat Street
London SW1P 1PH
020 7306 9606
e-mail: enquiries@alzheimers.org.uk

Crossroads Association

10 Regent Place
Rugby
Warwickshire CV1 2PN
0845 450 0350

Dementia Voice
The Dementia Services Development Centre for the South West
Blackberry Hill Hospital
Manor Road
Fishponds
Bristol BS16 2EW
0117 975 4863
Website: http://www.dementia-voice.org.uk
e-mail: office@demetia-voice.org.uk

Disabled Living Foundation
380–384 Harrow Road
London W9 2HU
0845 130 9177
Website: http://www.dlf.org.uk

Help the Aged
This organization works for a world in which older people are
valued for their contribution to society and can live fulfilled lives.
Regionally organized. Local addresses in Telephone Directories.
Website: http://www.helptheaged.org.uk

University of the Third Age
Main purpose is to encourage lifelong learning for those no
longer in full-time gainful employment.

Third Age Trust
19 East Street
Bromley
Kent BR1 1QH.
020 8466 6139
Website: http://www.u3a.org.uk

Christian-based Organizations that are Working for the General Good of Society

Christian Council on Ageing
Good list of helpful publications

Epworth House
Stuart Street
Derby DE1 2EQ
Website: http://freespace.virgin.net/milee.lowis/CCOA/

Christian Council on Ageing Dementia Group
c/o The Chaplaincy Centre
St Nicholas Hospital
Gosforth
Newcastle upon Tyne NE3 3XT

Church Army
Marlow House
109 Station Road
Sidcup
Kent DA15 7AD
020 8309 9991
Website: http://www.churcharmy.org.uk
e-mail: info@churcharmy.org.uk

Department of Christian Responsibility & Citizenship
Roman Catholic Boards of Social Responsibility
39 Eccleston Square
London SW1V 1BX
020 7901 4828
Website: http://www.dayforlife.org
e-mail: dayforlife@cbcew.org.uk

Leveson Centre for the Study of Ageing, Spirituality and Social Policy
Temple Balsall
Knowle
Solihull
West Midlands B93 0AL

Methodist Homes for the Aged
Centre of Spirituality and Ageing
Epworth House
Stuart Street
Derby DE1 2EQ
01332 296 200
e-mail: spirituality@mha.org.uk

Centre for Spirituality and Ageing
MHA Care Group
Chaplaincy & Spirituality
Epworth House
Stuart Street
Derby DE1 2EQ
01132 796 200
e-mail: spirituality@mha.org.uk

Psalm
An organization set up jointly by Church Army and C of E
Diocese of Edmonton, for developing opportunities for continuing work and ministry by, and work for, older people in the
Edmonton´ Episcopal Area.

6 Sandwich Street
London WC1H 9PL
020 77388 1461
Website: http://www.psalm.org.uk
e-mail: PSALM@stpancraschurch.org

St Columba's Fellowship
A Christian Presence in the Hospice Movement

4 Roebuck Bungalows
Kettlewell
Skipton
North Yorkshire BD23 5RE
01756 760452
Website: http://www.stcolumbasfellowship.com
e-mail: pauline@stcolumbasfellowship.com

Islamic Organization
The Islamic Foundation
Markfield Conference Centre
Ratby Lane
Markfield
Leicestershire LE67 9SY
01530 244944
Website: http://www.islamic-foundation.org.uk